The Secret Life of Angels

RON RHODES

HARVEST HOUSE PUBLISHERS
EUGENE, OREGON

Unless otherwise indicated, all Scripture quotations are taken from the HOLY BIBLE, NEW INTERNATIONAL VERSION®. NIV®. Copyright © 1973, 1978, 1984 by the International Bible Society. Used by permission of Zondervan. All rights reserved.

Verses marked KJV are taken from the King James Version of the Bible.

Cover by Dugan Design Group, Bloomington, Minnesota

Cover photo © vichly4thai, Ig0rZh / Fotolia

Formerly Titled *Angels Among Us*
THE SECRET LIFE OF ANGELS

Published by Harvest House Publishers
Eugene, Oregon 97402
www.harvesthousepublishers.com

Library of Congress Cataloging-in-Publication Data
Rhodes, Ron.
[Angels among us]
The secret life of angels / Ron Rhodes.
pages cm
Includes bibliographical references.
ISBN 978-0-7369-4879-1 (pbk.)
ISBN 978-0-7369-4880-7 (eBook)
1. Angels—Christianity. I. Title.
BT966.3.R5 2014
235'.3—dc23

2013043546

Printed in the United States of America

15 16 17 18 19 20 21 22 / LB-SK / 10 9 8 7 6 5 4 3

This book is lovingly dedicated to my grandmother,

Annie Belle Carothers.

Away from the body, at home with the Lord.

Acknowledgments

A special thanks to my wife, Kerri, for proofreading each chapter in this book prior to publication. I so appreciate her assistance and encouragement. Thanks also to our children David and Kylie—my personal cheering squad.

To all my friends at Harvest House Publishers—working with you is a pleasure. Blessings to you all!

Contents

From the Voices of Angels

Patmos is a mountainous desert island located on the Aegean Sea and covers about 60 square miles. Rome exiled criminals to this desolate island, and this is where Domitian, the emperor of Rome, exiled the aged apostle John as a punishment for sharing the good news of Jesus Christ with everyone he met. John was sent here to die of either old age or starvation.

Little did John know what God had in store for him on this tiny, secluded island. Sometime around AD 90—about 60 years after Jesus had risen from the dead and ascended to heaven—John had the most sweeping and panoramic vision any saint of God ever received. John was privileged to behold Christ in His awesome postresurrection glory.

During this incredible vision, John witnessed innumerable angels singing a song of worship to the Messiah, Jesus Christ:

> I looked and heard the voice of many angels, numbering thousands upon thousands, and ten thousand times ten thousand. They encircled the throne and the

> living creatures and the elders. In a loud voice they sang: "Worthy is the Lamb, who was slain, to receive power and wealth and wisdom and strength and honor and glory and praise!" (Revelation 5:11-12).

"Ten thousand times ten thousand" is a lot of angels. In fact, this calculates to 100 million angels surrounding Christ on the throne and singing a magnificent worship song in praise of Him.

To give you a perspective regarding how many angels this is, the average football stadium in America holds about 50,000 people. It would take 2000 stadiums of that size to hold 100,000,000 people. Such large numbers boggle the mind!

Actually, the total number of angels John saw may far exceed 100 million. I say this because "ten thousand" was the highest numerical figure used in the Greek language.[1] "Ten thousand times ten thousand" may be John's way of describing an inexpressibly large company of angels—myriads upon myriads.

Try to imagine the scene. This magnificent company of at least 100 million angels—with every single one radiating resplendent, luminous beauty—surrounds Christ's glorious throne and sings praises to His matchless name. The sound of this many voices singing in unison to Christ must surely have been the most awe-inspiring experience John (or any other human) ever encountered. What a precious privilege God gave His lowly servant!

Bible expositor John MacArthur exults in this majestic praise song: "I cannot wait to hear it. I cannot wait to sing it with a glorified voice, and be part of the great chorus of the redeemed, with the entire host of heaven joining in."[2] MacArthur expresses a longing in every Christian's heart!

Note that this majestic worship scene ascribes power, glory, and honor to Jesus Christ (Revelation 5:12). These are the exact words used to describe the worship of the Father in Revelation 4:11. Jesus receives from this vast company of angels the same worship as the Father!

Why do I begin a book on angels in this way? Simply because I want to set the tone for the rest of the book. Many recent books focus on angels as an end in themselves, completely (or largely) apart from God. This is not as it should be.

Angels exist because Christ created them to exist (Colossians 1:16). Angels exist as eternal servants to God and Christ (Psalm 103:20). Any discussion of angels that treats them as an end in themselves is unbalanced.

In chapter 1 we will consider some testimonies of people who claim to have had a close encounter of the celestial kind—that is, an encounter with an angel. Then, in chapters 2 through 4, we'll focus attention on some of the imbalances that have emerged in recent years regarding angels. Throughout the rest of the book, we will zero in on what the Bible tells us about this intriguing subject.

As you discover what Scripture has to say, I am confident you will begin to grasp the glorious provisions God has made for our care and well-being in the world. You will see that angels are indeed among us.

PART 1

Close Encounters of the Celestial Kind

Millions of spiritual creatures walk the earth unseen, both when we wake, and when we sleep; All these with ceaseless praise his works behold both day and night.

~ John Milton ~

1

Angels in the World Today

Sally, a woman who attends my church, could not restrain her tears as she poured out her heart to Pastor Dave. After a series of medical tests, Sally's doctor had called to inform her that the baby she was expecting would be born with Down syndrome. Pastor Dave shared Sally's grief at the news. He vowed to help Sally and her husband, Jim, in any way he could.[1]

The following day Pastor Dave decided to send Sally and Jim a postcard with a word of encouragement. On the card, Dave assured them of how much God loved them and their soon-to-be-born little baby.

The postcard was delivered to a wrong address several miles from Sally and Jim's house. Sue—who lived at the house the card was mistakenly delivered to—decided to take the postcard to Sally personally.

When Sally opened the door, Sue said, "This card from your pastor was delivered to my house by mistake. I wanted to come by and deliver the card personally because I too have a child with Down syndrome, and I want to help you through this if you'll let me. God has shown me so much that I would like to share with you."

Did the God of all comfort send one of His angels to reroute the mail to Sue's house? We can't know for sure, but it seems a good possibility. Skeptics would tell us this was just a freak accident, but I see the supernatural at work here.

Angels are real. Angels are alive. And though we rarely perceive their presence, they are very much with us here on the earth.

Christians have always believed in angels. We can easily understand why. After all, the same Bible that attests to the reality and activity of God among His people likewise attests—with equal vigor—to the reality and activity of angels in our world. Scripture testifies to innumerable angels, all active in some capacity in carrying out the bidding of God.

In recent years, many believers have spoken of actual encounters with angels. Many of these reports come from quite reliable sources and have the ring of authenticity. As you read the following accounts, I think you will begin to see why I originally entitled this book *Angels Among Us*.

Escort into Glory

Evangelist Billy Graham reports that when his maternal grandmother died, the room seemed to fill with a heavenly light. "She sat up in bed and almost laughingly said, 'I see Jesus. He has His arms outstretched toward me. I see Ben [her husband who had died some years earlier] and I see the angels.' She slumped over, absent from the body but present with the Lord."[2]

Revival in a Hospital

The editor of *Leadership* magazine, a popular publication

among church leaders, speaks of how his young daughter was comatose one night, very near death. *Christianity Today* magazine reported that a hospital staff worker stopped by the room and witnessed an astonishing sight—angels were hovering over the girl's bed.

By the following morning, the daughter had amazingly revived. This editor—not prone to sensationalism—does not hesitate to believe that angels had truly visited his girl that night.[3] The staff worker renewed her commitment to God as a result of the incredible sight she had seen.

Rescue on the Missionary Field

Reverend John G. Paton was a missionary in the New Hebrides Islands. According to his testimony, his mission headquarters was surrounded by hostile natives one night. They apparently intended to burn the building to the ground and put John and his wife to death.

The Patons turned to God, throwing themselves on His mercy and asking Him to deliver them. They prayed throughout the night, and when the first rays of sunlight came the next morning, the Patons were utterly amazed to see that the natives had left.

About a year later, the chief of that tribe became a Christian. When Paton asked the chief why the tribe had refrained from burning down the headquarters on that fateful night, the chief surprised him by inquiring, "Who were all those men you had there with you?"

Paton answered, "There were no men there—just my wife and I."

The chief then told Paton that he and his warriors had seen hundreds of men standing guard outside the headquarters that night—all dressed in shining garments with swords drawn. These guards completely encircled the headquarters, and the tribe dared not attack.

Paton then realized that God had dispatched His angels to guard him and his wife.[4] As Psalm 34:7 tells us, "The angel of the LORD encamps around those who fear him, and he delivers them." Moreover, "He will command his angels concerning you to guard you in all your ways" (Psalm 91:11).

Paton's testimony sounds remarkably similar to the story of Elisha in 2 Kings 6:15-17. In this story, Elisha and his servant were surrounded by hostile forces, but they were not alone.

> When the servant of the man of God got up and went out early the next morning, an army with horses and chariots had surrounded the city. "Oh, my lord, what shall we do?" the servant asked. "Don't be afraid," the prophet answered. "Those who are with us are more than those who are with them." And Elisha prayed, "O LORD, open his eyes so that he may see." Then the LORD opened the servant's eyes, and he looked and saw the hills full of horses and chariots of fire all around Elisha.

Protection for Children in the Congo

Corrie ten Boom tells of an event that occurred during a rebellion in the Congo. Some rebels had advanced on a school where about 200 missionary children lived. "They planned to kill both children and teachers," she said. "In the school, they knew of the danger and therefore went to prayer. Their only protection was a fence and a couple of soldiers, while the enemy, who came closer and closer, amounted to several hundred."

Incredibly, as soon as the rebels came close by, they suddenly turned around and bolted away! The exact same thing happened the next day and the day after that when the rebels tried to approach the school.

One of the rebels was wounded and was brought to the missionary hospital. As the doctor was dressing his wounds, he asked the rebel, "Why did you not break into the school as you planned?"

The rebel responded, "We could not do it. We saw hundreds of soldiers in white uniforms, and we became scared."

Corrie later reflected that "in Africa, soldiers never wear white uniforms. So it must have been angels. What a wonderful thing that the Lord can open the eyes of the enemy so that they see angels!"[5]

Rescue at a Dark Intersection

Micki Stella was a Christian missionary who participated in evangelistic crusades in Korea. An evangelistic meeting ended late one night, and she and other missionaries were being driven to their homes. Her home was more out of the way than the others, so she volunteered to be dropped off at a normally busy intersection, where she would hail a taxi to her home.

Micki had visited this location only during the daylight hours. During the day, it seemed a safe environment. Standing there at night, she soon realized it was potentially dangerous. The intersection was all but deserted at night except for some men apparently doing some heavy drinking. As well, the taxis that frequented the area during the day were conspicuously absent.

A group of five men who had been in a nearby tavern were now out on the street, stumbling around and being noisy. One broke away from the group and started toward her, his arms extended in front of him. He said, "Come with me for one minute."

Micki, her eyes widening, started walking, looking for an escape. She was fearful of going farther down the dark street, but the man's four friends blocked the sidewalk in the other direction. "No. I don't want to go with you," she blurted out. She began to panic as the man continued toward her. She felt trapped. Here is her testimony:

> Suddenly, a large Korean man appeared from the alley leading to the open-air market. He walked deliberately in our direction. What immediately struck me was that he was so different from any Korean man I had seen in my dozen years in Korea to that time. He was *big*—a really burly-looking man—whereas Korean men of that time were almost always short and slight of build. Immediately I just knew he had come to help me! My fear was replaced by a very strange sense of peace. He walked to a point between me and my would-be assailant and just stood there as solid as a rock.
>
> The drunken man looked at him and came to the same conclusion—this man was my protector. He stopped in his tracks, then turned to go with his friends, who had already begun to walk away. I watched him just long enough to see that he was gone for good, then turned to thank my protector, who had not spoken a word. *No one was there. This is impossible,* I thought. I called to him. There was no answer. I even walked further down the dark street to the alley and called into that black hole which was normally a busy market, but heard no response.[6]

Emergency Guidance on the Road

Marlene Wiechman, a 33-year-old mother in West Point, Nebraska, believes angels rendered assistance when her six-year-old daughter's health took a drastic turn for the worse: "Emily had had a stroke at seven months, and she's partially handicapped," Wiechman says. Years later, Emily became ill while the family was vacationing.

> Last year, we went on vacation with my parents to Yellowstone National Park. On the way home, driving through Wyoming, Emily said she didn't feel well. She started vomiting, and her eyes weren't focusing. We needed to get her to a hospital, but the nearest town, Rock Springs, was 70 miles away.
>
> Emily kept getting worse, and as we approached Rock Springs, I prayed we would find help quickly. Just then, we saw a blue-and-white hospital sign. There were three or four more signs that led us straight to the emergency room.

A doctor at the hospital was able to quickly diagnose Emily as having a seizure and was able to stabilize her with anticonvulsants. When the moment of crisis was over, Ms. Wiechman mentioned that the signs had been a lifesaver.

> The doctor looked at me and said, "What signs?" He said he traveled that road every day, and there were no hospital signs. But all four adults in our van had seen them. We went back and looked again. They were gone. I called someone at the chamber of commerce, who said there had never been any hospital signs on that route. I believe they were put there for us by God or his angels.[7]

Companion on a Dangerous Mountain

A Christian missionary in Norway believes an angel assisted him on a dangerous mountain. To reach families living in his valley, he had to descend a dangerous mountain trail. At one steep, dangerous place, he stopped to pray, asking God to protect him with His angels. He safely reached the valley without harm.

At the first cottage the missionary met a man with his wife who had been watching his descent of the dangerous trail. "What has become of your companion?" they asked.

"What companion?" the missionary responded.

"The man who was with you," they exclaimed in surprise. "We were watching you as you came down the mountain, and it really seemed to us that there were two men crossing the mountain together."

"Then," reported the missionary, "I was reminded of my prayer to God for help, and of the word of the Lord in Psalm 34:7, 'The angel of the LORD encampeth round about them that fear him, and delivereth them.' "[8]

Rescue from a Train Disaster

Respected Bible expositor A.C. Gaebelein speaks of an incident in which he is convinced an angel sent from God rescued him and his companions from sure disaster. While traveling on a train, Gaebelein and his friends committed themselves into God's loving hands for a safe trip. Strangely, they sensed danger in their hearts that night, but they nevertheless trusted in God for safety.

They slept through that night peacefully. When they awoke the next morning, they were informed of a near tragedy that had occurred during the night:

> The train was hours late and the crew told us that near to midnight the train had been flagged by a farmer and had been brought to a stop less than five yards from a deep abyss. A storm further north sent its floodwaters down the creek and washed the wooden bridge away. A farmer was asleep. He said a voice awoke him to arise. He heard the rushing water and hastily dressed himself and lit a lantern, when he heard the oncoming train, which he stopped in time.[9]

Gaebelein has always believed that the voice that awoke the farmer that night was nothing less than an angel of God. He wonders how many other times in his life he has been rescued from danger without even knowing danger was present.

Rescue from a Burning Room

One day in 1977 Linda Gates of Sacramento, California, was cleaning her kitchen when she suddenly heard her four-year-old boy, Michael, running down the hall. She then heard the front door slam shut—an unusual occurrence because the door was warped and required adult strength to close tightly. Going outside, Linda found Michael, his eyes wide. He said, "A man got me out, Mama! A man got me out!"

Michael then led his mother to his smoke-filled room, where a curtain was burning. As it turned out, Michael had been playing with a box of matches and set the curtains on fire. After firefighters put out the blaze, one of them told Linda the smoke could easily have killed her son.

Linda recounts, "Michael told me that a man with long blond hair and a 'many-colored' shirt had appeared at his door and said, 'Michael, come out of there.' When my son said he wanted to look for his teddy bear, the man pulled him out of the room."

That evening their bedtime story just happened to be about Daniel and the lions' den, where they read, "My God sent his angel, and he shut the mouths of the lions. They have not hurt me, because I was found innocent in his sight" (Daniel 6:22). Linda was confident God had sent His angel to rescue her son.[10]

God's Heavenly Helpers

Were bona fide angels really involved in each of the above cases? They all have the ring of authenticity, but only God knows for sure. One thing is clear. Each of the above cases illustrates in a graphic way what Scripture has to say about the role of angels: "Are not all angels ministering spirits sent to serve those who will inherit salvation?" (Hebrews 1:14).

The root meaning of the word *ministering* has to do with rendering service. God created the angels to render service in various capacities. Popular Bible expositor Ray Stedman says that angelic ministry may involve protection (Psalm 91:11), guidance (Genesis 19:16-17), encouragement (Judges 6:12), deliverance (Acts 12:7), supply (Psalm 105:40), enlightenment (Matthew 2:19-20), and empowerment (Luke 22:43).[11]

Later we will see that angels are also involved in other kinds of service not specifically related to Christians. Some angels render service directly to God and Christ. Other angels bring judgment against unbelievers. We will see that angels are involved in carrying out the sovereign bidding of God in many different ways.

There is an increasing conviction that Gabriel and his friends are intervening in our everyday lives—with an arm to block our way as we absent-mindedly step out into oncoming traffic, a friendly push towards our perfect partner, or even a bag of gold.

~ Laura Davis ~

2

Flying High: The Popularity of Angels

Angels were once relegated mainly to Christmas cards and manger scenes, but not anymore. Angels have thoroughly infiltrated the popular culture! From mainline Christians to people of a wide variety of religious persuasions, many today seek comfort from these heavenly helpers in a troubled and often chaotic world.[1]

Of course, angels have been the subject matter of popular songs for decades. Hit songs in the angel genre include "Earth Angel," "Angel Eyes," "Johnny Angel," "Next Door to an Angel," "Where Angels Fear to Tread," and "My Special Angel." One reporter estimated that one in every ten pop songs mentions an angel.[2]

In the 1990s, the angel movement exploded on the scene and catapulted angels directly into the mainstream of American society. Some of today's biggest magazines ran feature cover stories on angels, including *Time, Newsweek, Ladies Home Journal,* and *Redbook.* As well, major television networks ran prime-time specials featuring angels.

The angelmania of the 1990s gave rise to the emergence of angel-only boutiques, angel-only specialty stores and catalog houses, angel calendars, angel postcards, angel T-shirts, angel sunglasses, angel newsletters, angel seminars, angel workshops, angel focus groups, angel sections at mainstream bookstores, and courses on angels at major universities and seminaries—including Harvard Divinity School.[3]

In its cultural commentary on the 1990s angel movement, written in 1993, *Newsweek* magazine observed that "angels are appearing everywhere in America" and that "those who see angels, talk to them, and put others in touch with them are prized guests on television and radio talk shows."[4] During those days, people claimed that "'getting in touch with your inner angel' will help solve your problems, from relationship woes to addiction."[5] The general mind-set was that angels could cure just about anything.

Understandably, a deluge of angel books flooded the marketplace, including popular books by Joan Wester Anderson, Terry Lynn Taylor, Eileen Freeman, and Sophy Burnham. Joan Wester Anderson's 1992 book, *Where Angels Walk: True Stories of Heavenly Visitors,* spent more than a year on the *New York Times* bestseller list and has been reprinted in at least 14 languages. The book has sold millions of copies.[6]

Most of these authors have continued to write angel books in more recent years, including Sophy Burham's *A Book of Angels* (2005), Terry Lynn Taylor's *Messengers of Love, Light, and Grace* (2005), and Joan Wester Anderson's *Guardian Angels: True Stories of Answered Prayers* (2006). Each of these books has enjoyed vigorous sales.

The media's angelmania of the 1990s has waned, but angels are more popular than ever. A Gallup poll revealed that 72 percent of Americans claimed to believe in angels in 1994, increasing to 78 percent in 2004. This same poll indicated that as of 2004, 84 percent of women believed in angels as opposed to 72 percent of men.[7] In 2005, a Fox news poll revealed that 79 percent of Americans believed in angels, with women more likely to believe than men (86 percent versus 72 percent).[8]

More recently, in December 2006, an Associated Press–AOL News poll revealed that a whopping 81 percent of Americans, almost regardless of backgrounds and religious convictions, think angels are real.

This means that while the angelmania of the 1990s has waned, the number of people in the general population who believe in angels has actually increased. Type the word *angel* into Google, and you'll see nearly 200 million links.

The Associated Press–AOL News poll also found that "belief in angels, however people define them, is highest—almost universal—among white evangelical Christians, 97 percent of whom trust in their existence...But even among people with no religious affiliation, well more than half said angels are for real." The poll further found that "Protestants, women, Southerners, Midwesterners and Republicans were the most likely to believe in angels, although strong majorities in other groups also shared that faith."[9]

Understanding Angel Popularity

Why are angels so popular today? What is causing more and more people in our society to believe in angels?

Of course, Christians are excited about angels because angelology is a biblical doctrine. Their interest in angels reflects their greater interest in Scripture. Others, however, have become excited about angels for all the wrong reasons and have bought into wildly unbiblical misconceptions about angels. Here are some of the off-base reasons angels are so popular among these people:

Misconception: Angels bring meaning and purpose into our lives. Angels make life worth living and provide unconditional happiness, fun, mirth, excitement, and success. They can help get rid of all the worry that plagues our lives. They're heaven-sent messengers who can help us create heaven on earth.[10] Wrong!

Misconception: Angels offer humankind a form of spirituality that does not necessarily demand a total commitment to God or His laws. A person can have a spiritual life by relating primarily to the angels without having to worry about (for example) obeying God's Ten Commandments. Angels are kind, compassionate, and nonjudgmental. They always accept us just the way we are. If people want a spirituality that doesn't necessarily involve God or Jesus, or if people want a spirituality that doesn't involve having to hold to specific theological doctrines, then angels are the ticket![11] Wrong!

Misconception: Angels can make us feel loved. One angel enthusiast affirmed, "Their connection with me is one of love, comfort, and security. On three different occasions I have actually felt them all hug me, not as we know hugging, with arms, but an embrace with their whole being; and I feel tingly and a surge of pure electrical love runs throughout my whole body."[12] People need this kind of love today, and the angels are happy to oblige. Wrong!

Misconception: Angels can empower us to accomplish great tasks. After all, "with God and his angels, nothing…is impossible."[13] One angel enthusiast boasts, "Whenever I think my mission impossible, the angels venture forward to lead the way."[14] Wrong!

Misconception: Angels recognize our divinity. One of the

main messages angels have for us is that "we are God on earth." "We are God. God is us."[15] Wrong!

Misconception: Angels have stepped up their activity among us in recent years in order to help us. Angels are aware that these are troubled and painful times for many human beings. Angels are therefore here to help us resolve such ills as homelessness, hunger, physical and emotional sickness, and the destruction of the environment.[16] Wrong!

Misconception: Guardian angels render protection for all people (regardless of religious beliefs) in an often threatening world. The world is a dangerous place to live, with rising crime rates in all the major cities. Societal problems seem insurmountable. Terrorism is on the rise. Guardian angels are stepping up their activities among us because people are scared and know they need protection. The idea that a powerful celestial being is watching over each of us—regardless of our religious beliefs—is a very comforting thought for many, but wrong.[17]

Misconception: Angels provide a spiritual balance to Western society's overemphasis on materialism and secularism. Many who have cast their lot with the angels say it has become easier to believe in celestial beings as we see evidence that high technology cannot solve all of society's ills. Science is not the answer to everything.[18] The angels have answers and solutions that meet many of our needs. The angels can succeed where technology fails. "Few people think anymore that all of life's important answers can be found in science and rational thought and reasonable logic. They know reality has another dimension—a spiritual dimension beyond science and reason. And this 'other' side of reality keeps growing bigger in popular thought."[19] One analyst has suggested that "as science, technology, and rational explanations uncover and explain more and more about the known world, Americans are...becoming more intrigued by the unknown"[20]—especially the world of angels.

Misconception: Angels give assurance to all people regarding life after death. Many angels today have supposedly informed people that no one need fear death, for death is just a gateway into the next (more exalted) level of existence.[21] One's religious preference does not matter. The same wonderful destiny awaits us all. Wrong!

Impostors Among Us?

By now you can see that the excitement many have about angels today is rooted in wildly unbiblical ideas. We will touch on even wilder perspectives about angels in the next two chapters and will see more evidence that much of what today's angel enthusiasts teach has little to do with the heavenly helpers described in the pages of the Bible.

In fact, much of what is being taught about angels today in some of the bestselling books would seem to have more to do with *fallen* angels (demons) than God's holy angels. These fallen angels are impostors who pose as benevolent helpers of humankind but who foster a spirituality without Christ and without God (2 Corinthians 11:14-15).

With angel mail, you write your special request on a piece of paper and mail it to the angels…Thank the angels as if the request has already been granted.

~ Terry Lynn Taylor ~

3

Celestial Quackery, Part 1: Making Contact with Angels

The first edition of this book was published in 1994, at the height of the angel movement that swept across this country like a tidal wave. Among the primary—and, I might add, *strange*—interests of people at that time was how to make contact with angels, understanding the various ways angels can appear to humans, angelic messages from the great beyond, the aftereffects of angel visitations, and the alleged benefits of angel contact.

When I decided to revise the book in 2007, I was curious to see if angel enthusiasts were still expressing some of the same bizarre ideas that were prevalent back in the 1990s. To my surprise, the answer is largely yes, though to be sure, I found some differences in emphasis. In this chapter and the next, I will focus attention on the "celestial quackery" that continues to remain part and parcel of the religious landscape in America, citing important resources from both the 1990s and the 2000s.

Making Contact with Angels

That contact with angels would become a matter of concern to Americans in modern times seems almost inconceivable. But indeed, it *has* become a matter of concern—and in a very big way. I have read literally dozens of angel books that promote different methods and ideas about how to make contact with angels. And as we will see, quite a number of these methods and ideas involve mysticism and various forms of occultism.

Several angel writers over the past few decades speak of the need for mystical intuition that enables us to sense the presence of angels. For example, Terry Lynn Taylor, author of *Messengers of Light: The Angels' Guide to Spiritual Growth* (1990), said that "to get to know angels, it helps if you can transcend the 'seeing is believing' paradigm and adopt an open mind and a stance of 'knowing by intuition.' "[1] More recently (2005), we find Taylor singing the same tune: "Pay attention to your intuition…for it is through the inner knowing of intuition that you receive messages from your guardian angel to warn and guide you." She claims, "The main source I have used for all of the books I have written has been my strong intuitions regarding angels."[2]

No wonder such a wide diversity of strange ideas about angels is floating around out there. When people depart from the objective truth recorded in God's Word, the Bible, and replace it with mystical intuition, the door is wide open for new ideas to come from "the other side."

What about occultism? In the 1990s, Alma Daniel, Timothy Wyllie, and Andrew Ramer, in their book *Ask Your Angels,* claimed to contact angels through Eastern meditation, visualization, breath control, exercises with chakras (alleged energy centers in the human body), tuning into angel frequencies, channeling, and divination.[3] Jane Howard, in her book *Commune with the Angels,* likewise claimed that "through [Eastern] meditation, prayer, and psychic development exercises, we can become fluent in seeing, hearing, and sensing members of other kingdoms. When we use our superphysical sense of sight to develop our clairvoyancy, we are able to see the angels face to face."[4] (*Clairvoyance* literally means "clear seeing." It involves the occultic ability to see something beyond natural means into the spirit world, whether relating to the past, present, or future.)

More recently, Sophy Burnham speaks about how her involvement in occultism helps her perceive angels and other paranormal entities: "I suppose you cannot meet an apparition without having other psychic experiences: telepathy, clairvoyance, ESP." She acknowledges, "These days I see angels easily. I see auras...I give psychic or intuitive readings...As a seer, I can hold an object belonging to someone, go into a slightly altered state, and know a lot about that person's past and present and, to some degree, the choices they face in the future."[5] So for Burnham, angel contact is just part and parcel of her involvement in the broader world of the occult.

A number of famous angel authors today display a heavy dependency on other authors or thinkers who are heavily involved either in occultism, cultism, or various false religions. For example, in Sophy Burnham's 2004 book, *A Book of Angels,* she cites Mary Baker Eddy (the founder of the Christian Science cult), the Buddha, Meister Eckhart (a famous mystic), Emanuel Swedenborg (the founder of Swedenborgianism, another cult), Paramahansa Yogananda (who was instrumental in bringing Kriya Yoga to the West), Rudolf Steiner (the founder of the Anthroposophy cult), and Annie Besant (the leader of the Theosophical Society, another cult). Swedenborg, Steiner, and Besant in particular were all heavily involved in various forms of occultism and especially psychic contact with spirit entities.

In Terry Lynn Taylor's recent books, she cites such prominent figures as Jiddu Krishnamurti (proclaimed at one time to be the new incarnation of the Maitreya Buddha by the Theosophical Society), the Dalai Lama (the leader of Tibetan Buddhism), occultist Manly P. Hall (the author of many occult books), New Age forerunner and mythology expert Joseph Campbell, controversial New Age leader Matthew Fox (who penned *The Coming of the Cosmic Christ*), New Age author James Redfield (who wrote *The Celestine Prophecy*), New Age author Gary Zukav (author of *The Seat of the Soul*), Paramahansa Yogananda, and Mahatma Gandhi. With such a heavy dependency on such religious thinkers, we should not be surprised that many of the ideas about angels in Taylor's and Burnham's very popular books are patently unbiblical.

In the pages ahead, I will touch on some examples of mystical and occultic methodology for contacting angels. Along the way, you will come to see that the title of this chapter, "Celestial Quackery," is not an exaggeration.

In this chapter and the next, we will *not* investigate a thorough Christian response to each of the strange ideas mentioned—though I will occasionally cite a Bible verse to refute an idea. We will address the biblical view of angels throughout the rest of the book.[6]

Contacting Angels in the 1990s

Before exploring methods of angel contact common to both the 1990s and 2000s, let's briefly look at two methods that were apparently unique to the 1990s. So far as I have been able to determine, these methods of angel contact are no longer in wide use today. They nevertheless bear mentioning to demonstrate the depth of recent celestial quackery.

Color-coordinated wardrobe. John Ronner, author of *Do You Have a Guardian Angel?* claimed in the 1990s that one good method of hailing an angel "is to color-coordinate your wardrobe.

According to this far-out idea, soft green clothes will lure in guardian angels of the home, and deep sapphire blue will get the attention of healing angels."[7] Many angels enthusiasts believed that guardian angels like rose or pink and soft green; healing angels like deep sapphire blue; seraphim angels like crimson red; cherubim angels like blue; the archangel Michael likes deep green, vivid blue, gold, and rose; and Gabriel is attracted to tans, browns, and dark greens. These people believed that by wearing specific colors, they could attract specific kinds of angels into their lives.

Crystals charged with angel energy. Jane Howard claimed that a "cherubic crystal" can be of great benefit for a person seeking contact with angels.

> A cherubic crystal is one that you have activated in meditation and which has been charged by the Cherubim...Once you have selected the crystal, hold it between the palms of your hands. Ask out loud for the wisdom vibration emanated by the Cherubim to flow through you and into your hands so that the stone will become charged with the Cherubim's vibration. Prepare the crystal once in this manner and you will never have to do it again, unless someone tampers with it or changes its programming.[8]

Howard claims that when she holds her cherubic crystal, she can feel it become warm as angels "charge" and "bless" it. She also claims she can use several "activated crystals" to work with the "different choirs" of the angelic realm.[9] She says these activated crystals are especially beneficial in hospital rooms, for they attract many angels that can facilitate rapid healing.

Of course, nothing is wrong with a Christian owning a crystal. After all, crystals are pretty rocks created by God. However, the New Age use of crystals described above is a form of occultism, which God condemns (Deuteronomy 18:10-12).

Contacting Angels Today

Channeling

In the 1990s, New Age channeling was big. In this occultic practice, a seer or medium acts as a mouthpiece so that angels (or other spirit entities) can communicate to people on earth. Alma Daniel, Timothy Wyllie, and Andrew Ramer have long claimed that channeling is one of the best means for making angel contact. In their 1992 book they suggest an analogy of a television set and ask us to imagine that *we* are the set.

> There are many channels or stations broadcasting. (In this case, *channel* refers to a voice, not to the person receiving it.) Until you open to the angels, the only channel you're likely to get on your set comes from your mind, from your ego...Once you tune into the angels, you may find yourself receiving other stations as well—voices of guides, extraterrestrials, and nature spirits.[10]

These authors were thoroughly convinced that a genderless angelic being named Abigrael was giving them instructions on a variety of matters through channeling. And just as they themselves made angel contact through channeling, they have long sought to help others accomplish the same thing through the techniques they teach at their New Age workshops.[11]

During these early years of the angel movement, many New Age seers offered their services as channelers or mediums so their clients could get in contact with their guardian angels for $200 to $500 per hour. The appeal for such channeling sessions, even though outrageously expensive, was that guardian angels supposedly had all kinds of great wisdom that could help people live more vibrant and successful lives.[12]

Also popular during the 1990s were "angel listenings." A typical angel-listening session was a 20- to 30-minute conversation between the counselee and his or her guardian angel speaking through a channeler or medium, who acted as a mouthpiece for the angel while in a deep trance. During the session, the client might see a glow of light as well as sense some kind of celestial presence in the room.[13] Counselees claim to receive specific instructions and wisdom from their guardian angels through this channeling experience.

We see less emphasis today on New Age seers and "angel listenings," but today's most famous psychic mediums regularly speak of their encounters and interactions with angels. For example, psychic medium John Edward speaks of angel encounters in his recent book *What If God Were the Sun?* and his audio CD *Understanding Your Angels.*[14] Psychic medium James van Praagh speaks of angel encounters in his recent books *Talking to Heaven: A Medium's Message of Life After Death, Heaven and Earth: Making the Psychic Connection,* and *Meditations with James Van Praagh.*[15] Psychic medium Sylvia Browne speaks of angel encounters in her recent books *Phenomenon: Everything You Need to Know About the Paranormal, Life on the Other Side: A Psychic's Tour of the Afterlife,* and *Spiritual Connections: How to Find Spirituality Throughout All the Relationships in Your Life.*[16]

Terry Lynn Taylor, in her 2005 book *Messengers of Love, Light, and Grace,* addresses the issue of contacting spirit entities via channeling and claims that "the angels' language is primarily one of symbols, colors, sounds, and feelings."[17] This is significant because psychics have long taught that spirit entities from the great beyond (that is, the spirits of dead people) typically communicate to the living through symbols, colors, sounds, and feelings.

John Edward, for example, says that what he receives from spirits in the great beyond is akin to "psychic sign language." He says the spirits communicate in symbols. The more fluent the psychic mediums become in understanding the symbols, Edward claims, the more easily they can understand what the spirits are seeking to communicate.[18] For example, if during a psychic reading Edward senses a tightness in his chest, he may interpret that as meaning that the person died from a heart attack. If he senses blackness in the chest area, he may interpret that as meaning that the person died of lung cancer.[19] Angels too, we are told, communicate from the great beyond through symbols.

Of course, from a biblical perspective, channeling and spiritism are off-limits for the Christian. Indeed, God detests channelers and spiritists: "Let no one be found among you... who is a medium or spiritist or who consults the dead. Anyone who does these things is detestable to the LORD" (Deuteronomy 18:10-12). Scripture also states that "Satan himself masquerades as an angel of light" (2 Corinthians 11:14). He is perfectly capable of impersonating both the spirits of dead people and benevolent angels—and he does so to lead people astray. Angel enthusiasts beware!

Prayer

Angel enthusiasts have long claimed that people can contact angels through prayer. "Prayer is a way to communicate with the angels."[20] We can all "pray to angels to ask for their help and intercession in human affairs."[21] Indeed, "prayer is the way we talk to angels...When you pray to the angels, pray as if 'it is already done'; in other words, thank the angels in advance for taking care of your burdens."[22]

We can allegedly speak to the angels just as if they are our friends: "After you have become angel conscious, you will want to communicate with the angels in your own special way. Some people simply converse with the angels as if they were sitting in the room with a friend."[23] We should pray to the angels at first waking in the morning and daily affirm, "I know that unseen forces are always there to answer my requests and reward me with the unexpected."[24] We can even find emotional healing in our prayers to angels.[25]

We can also allegedly invoke the presence and activity of our guardian angels by praying a "Guardian Angel Prayer." It goes like this:

> Angel of God, my guardian dear;
> To whom His love commits me here;
> Ever this day, be at my side,
> To light and guard, to rule and guide.[26]

(Notice in all the above citations that prayer is directed toward angels and not to God. This directly violates scriptural instructions on prayer—see, for example, Matthew 6:9.)

Angel enthusiasts have also long taught that angels can make sure that whenever you choose to pray to God, your prayers will actually reach Him. "If you are someone who is concerned about God hearing your prayer 'down here,' trust in the angels' messenger service for a quick delivery of your prayer to God."[27]

Meditation

Meditation is another method of contacting angels that has been popular for quite some time. In the 1990s, Terry Lynn Taylor put it this way:

> Let your attention focus on angels. At this point, you may want to use the word *angel* as a form of mantra [a word that is mystically chanted over and over again]. Allow the word to take you wherever it will. Let a smile come over you, and notice the feeling of peace that comes with it. As you smile, feel yourself lifted and surrounded by white light. Ask the angels to lift you into heaven so that you can meet them.[28]

Taylor continues to teach similar ideas today. She recommends that you sit quietly in a comfortable, peaceful place and perhaps light a candle or some incense. Then close your eyes and relax. As you breathe, imagine that you are taking in light and that it is filling your soul. "Mentally ask that your guardian angel be part of your meditation; then let go of your mind...If you want to use the word *angel* as a mantra, allow the repeating of the word to bring you closer and closer to pure being and inner peace."[29] Such meditation, Taylor says, is immensely beneficial.

Angel enthusiasts tell us that as we develop skills in meditating, we can learn to tune in to the etheric realm, which is allegedly the realm of the angels. "Sometimes it's not a bad idea to 'pass out' and join them for a while, setting our earthly concerns aside and feeling the lightness and freedom of spirit they embody...In passing *out* of the physical realm we pass *into* the spiritual realm, where we feel and sense things more, not less, acutely."[30]

Meditation thus helps us attune to the spiritual world around us. "As we practice withdrawing our attention from the physical world and focusing it on the spiritual, our perception becomes less limited to materiality. The nonphysical realm becomes more real to us, and we develop the mental habit of attentiveness to it."[31] We are to keep in mind that "angels are always on call, and meditation is one of the best ways by which we can commune with them. Through meditation we can actually 'call up' the angels. Their number is listed and it's not a costly exchange. It's free and accessible to all, twenty-four hours a day."[32] And as we meditate and seek communion with the angels, they perpetually inspire us "by instilling ideas into our thought processes and patterns."[33]

Of course, the meditation described above is not biblical meditation. Biblical meditation—in contrast to the mysticism and emptying of the mind that is characteristic of Eastern meditation—involves objective contemplation and deep reflection on God's Word (Joshua 1:8) as well as His Person and faithfulness (Psalm 119; see also 19:14; 48:9; 77:12; 104:34; 143:5). Christians are called to biblical meditation, but they should avoid all forms of Eastern meditation.

Writing Letters

This may seem hard to believe, but for decades, angel enthusiasts have suggested that writing letters to angels is a great way to communicate with them. According to Daniel, Wyllie, and Ramer, all you have to do is "date your letter, write 'Dear Angel,' and just let your words flow. Ask for your angel's support and/or guidance and give thanks for its assistance in advance. Then sign it at the end as you would a letter to a friend."[34]

Once the letter is completed, these authors suggest, you can mail it by placing it in a Bible, on a meditation altar, or in a personal box where you keep special items. You can also mail it by putting it under a pillow when you go to bed at night. Yet another option is to burn the letter, "sending the message up to the heavens with the rising smoke."[35] Regardless of the delivery method you choose, you can rest assured the letter has been sent.

In the 1990s, Terry Lynn Taylor suggested that if you are having interpersonal problems with a particular person, you may want to consider writing that person's guardian angel a letter: "If there is someone in your life—your boss, your spouse, your child, your coworker, or your friend—with whom you have trouble communicating without disagreements and arguments over trivial issues, try writing to that person's guardian angel and ask that the situation be understood on the highest level."[36] You can be confident that "when you write to someone else's guardian, the message gets delivered on the angelic level."[37]

More recently (2005), Taylor has come up with some specific suggestions for increasing the effectiveness of writing letters to angels. She suggest that "to make a special request to the angels, simply take a piece of paper and address it to your own highest angel and the highest angels of the others your request involves." She advises that "in your request, be specific and define what it is you want as clearly as you can." She urges that one "always add the phrase 'for the highest good of all concerned' to your note." One should then close the letter by expressing gratitude: "Thank the angels as if the request has already been granted."[38]

A good number of angel enthusiasts believe that angels are fully capable of communicating back to us through letters. How so? All you need to do is "pick up another piece of paper...This time, start your letter by writing 'Dear ________,' and fill in your own name. Then relax and let your angel's words come through you in the form of a letter."[39] In other words, you can act as a channel through whom your guardian angel can write a letter to you. (In occultic circles this type of practice is known as automatic handwriting.)

Visualization

Visualization is yet another popular tool for alleged angel contact.[40] Popular angel author Sophy Burnham has long used guided imagery (or visualization) to help her workshop attendees make contact with angels. In a typical workshop, Burnham uses visualization and "guided meditation" to silence the mind and "unlock the imagination." Once in this mystical state, attendees listen for angel messages.[41]

Another angel enthusiast suggests this typical visualization exercise for making angel contact:

> In your mind's eye see a bridge appear before you—a bridge of light. Get up and walk across this bridge that leads you into the angelic realm. Don't be just a spectator and see yourself walking across the bridge—actually feel and imagine it as you get up and walk. Focus your awareness on walking across the bridge and, if you need to, say to yourself, "I am walking across the bridge with my Guardian Angel." Once on the other side of the bridge acknowledge that you have crossed over into the angelic realm.[42]

The Christian, of course, recognizes the danger of such guided imagery sessions. For one thing, the human imagination has been thoroughly marred by sin (Genesis 6:5; Romans 8:7; Ephesians 4:18). We are therefore using faulty equipment to begin with. Beyond this, we must recognize that guided imagery can induce an altered state of consciousness that can have extremely dangerous consequences. Christian specialists in the field of occultism have often warned that any kind of activity that leads to an altered state of consciousness can make a person vulnerable to demonic affliction.

In this chapter, we've seen several alleged methods of angel contact. In the next chapter, we'll look at claims regarding different ways angels can appear today, messages from angels, the aftereffects of angel contact, and the benefits of angel contact. All of this is celestial quackery.

[Angel appearances] come in the form in which they can be received: as dreams, accidents, coincidence, intuition—that tap on the shoulder that says "go there" and "don't go there."

~ Sophy Burnham ~

4

Celestial Quackery, Part 2: Angel Appearances Today

Angels appear in many ways, according to the current angelic pop literature. Much of this literature scores high on the celestial-quackery index.

For example, one recent angel enthusiast informs her readers, "You may see a streak of light or even a winged figure. You could experience sudden shivers running down your spine, a feeling of unexpected warmth, or a soft brush against your skin." She says "there may be a lingering fragrance of flowers or pine and you could hear a voice or the sound of beautiful music in your head." Other signs of angelic presence might include "tiny specks of glitter which sometimes attach themselves to people's faces or a white feather turning up in an unusual place."[1]

Angels supposedly can appear "as that little whisper at your shoulder saying, 'Don't go down that road.'" They can take the form of nudgings, intuition, or coincidence. They can appear as light on the water or in clouds and rainbows. They can even appear in the form of a swan.[2]

Angel enthusiasts claim that sometimes we see only their "ethereal, heavenly shadow," while at other times we only "feel their nearness" or perhaps "hear their whisper."[3] Sometimes we simply "feel the irresistible impulse to be cautious. Or we might feel a push to proceed." Angels often give us a "hunch, intuition, or premonition."[4]

Some claim that angels sometimes give us a "sudden surge of confidence" or a "flash of insight" or maybe a "sharp twinge of conscience."[5] An angel may pop an idea into your head, which may cause you to say, "It just dawned on me..."

We also read that angel appearances can be subtly disguised in everyday events. For example, "a child, in a moment of spontaneity, may blurt out a statement for which only you know the meaning." Or perhaps "while thumbing through a book, a page may fall open with a clear message in the print." Or "headlines in the newspaper, taken out of context, might contain your message."[6]

An angel might even communicate to you when you turn on the radio and hear lyrics in a song. One angel enthusiast reports, "The chorus of the song contained the words, 'I am going to be your soul provider.' I felt the words touch my heart and give me the reassurance that no matter what was uncertain in my life, I was going to have the support and love of my Guardian Angel. Together, we would be able to face anything."[7]

We also read that you might look out a window and see a truck drive by that has an angelic message for you. "As you look out the window, a truck goes by with words written on it that give you the answer you spent so much time trying to force out of your brain. As soon as you release the struggle, the message comes through effortlessly."[8]

One might wonder what governs the way an angel might appear. New Age author Sophy Burnham informs us that "these visitations and insights usually accord with the upbringing and conditioning of the recipient." The rule, she says, is that people receive only as much information as they can bear. As well, angel appearances "come in the form in which they can be received: as dreams, accidents, coincidence, intuition—that tap on the shoulder that says 'go there' and 'don't go there'...They come in books that we read or as animals (especially dogs, it seems) or as humans." Angel appearances seem to "take whatever form the visited person is willing to accept; and sometimes no form at all—a dream, a thought, a surge of power, a sense of guidance. They don't seem far removed from natural events. This explains why angels are easily explained away."[9]

Angelic Messages

Regardless of what form an angelic appearance might take, many today claim—contrary to the Bible—that the messages from angels are always positive. We read that a typical angelic message is, "Don't be afraid, everything is just fine. There is nothing but love."[10] Indeed, the angels urge us to accept that "we are love, we are God on earth, and it is time to love ourselves and open our hearts." Angels want you to know that "you are a divine being and that you are guided by a higher wisdom in the universe that operates for your highest good."[11]

Many also claim that angels want human beings to learn that truth is relative and that all the religions of the world are ultimately one. Angels allegedly look down on people who act as if they alone have all the answers to everyone's spiritual questions. We are encouraged to see the truth in all religious beliefs. Contrary to the exclusivist claims of Jesus Christ (John 14:6; see also Acts 4:12), angel enthusiasts say we should affirm with the angels, "I know that all spiritual roads ultimately lead to God."[12]

We read that God "shines in the heart of every person regardless of race, religion, location, or station in life. The Light doesn't change with the name or the rituals—the Light is the Light is the Light. Does sunlight change when it falls upon different faces? The sun remains the same; we are the receivers of its light, and we each have our own ways of facing its light."[13] The bottom line, then, is that we should not criticize others' religion.

The Aftereffects of Angelic Visitations

Angel enthusiasts describe the aftereffects of angelic visitations. Contrary to the Bible, they claim that angel visits "bring a calm and peaceful serenity that descends sweetly over you, and this is true even when the angel is not seen." Angels "always leave certain physical manifestations in their wake, something substantive to indicate that what witnesses have seen or felt was not just their imaginations. This may be as slight as a gladdening of the heart or a tingling in the fingertips." We may have "feelings of love, of greater self-acceptance, of inner peace, of being deeply cared for and recognized." Some claim we might even detect floral scents such as rose and jasmine.[14] Such things are allegedly clear indicators of angel visitations.

Alleged Benefits of Angelic Contact

Angel contact allegedly has a multitude of benefits. We read that people can receive guidance from angels, develop close friendships with them, get answers to important questions from them, learn to meditate better with their help, enlist their assistance in times of need, receive their help when going on a diet, develop angel healing groups in which humans get healed, and much, much more.[15] The benefits are seemingly endless. We'll consider some of these in greater detail and witness celestial quackery at its worst.

Angels Can Help Us Reach Our Goals

Angel enthusiasts claim we can team up with angels to accomplish our goals in life.[16] We can do this in any number of different ways. For example, we can make a "declaration" to angels that will help bring about what we desire in life. We openly announce to heaven what we want, declaring our goals and desires to the angels.[17] The angels will bless the declaration and bring about our wishes. (I don't know about you, but to me this sounds like a celestial form of "positive confession"—that is, angel-assisted "name it and claim it.")

Another way of attaining goals is to hold an "angel conference," clearly spelling out for the angels what we want to accomplish. They will then "act as your consultants and your staff of employees." Specific angels can be assigned to specific tasks.[18]

This supposed role of angels helping people to accomplish their goals in life is no doubt one reason for the current popularity of angels in the West.

Angels Can Help Us Evolve

According to Eileen Freeman, "The ancient servants of God and humanity [angels] have a mission, a God-given plan to help us grow in wisdom and love, not just so that we will survive as a race, but so we will be able to grow into what we were always intended to be—perfected beings capable of incredible energies and immense, transforming love."[19] By interacting with the angels, we can allegedly bring about powerful changes in our lives. Contact with the angels changes our consciousness and brings about spiritual transformation. The more we hang out with the angels, the more we are transformed. Biblically, of course, spiritual transformation comes through the Word of God (2 Timothy 3:15-17; see also Romans 12:2) and the ongoing ministry of the Holy Spirit (Galatians 5:16-25).

Angels Can Heal Us

Many angel enthusiasts believe angels are the source of physical, mental, and emotional healing energies. People can make an angel declaration of health and well-being that might include the following words: "I, [Your Name], formally and willingly choose to be open to the healing rays of Raphael the Archangel, whose name means Medicine of God. I ask that the angels under the guidance of Raphael shine the green rays of healing energy upon my being and into the depth of my soul."[20]

We are also told that angels can rearrange a person's cells on a microscopic level. They can allegedly program a person's immune system with healing messages and charge it up with energy.[21] They can bombard a person's body with healing rays, bringing the body to optimum health. So, we are urged, don't just go to the doctor, consult the angels!

Angels Can Bring Us Comfort

Sophy Burnham tells us that if we trust angels, they will "comfort us with invisible warm hands, and always they try to give us what we want."[22] As well, the angels can function as a cheering squad for our higher selves: "These angels cheer with little voices, 'Don't give up...We like who you are...Everything's going to be okay...We are proud of you.' "[23]

Many people also believe angels can help us eradicate worry in our lives. They act as "worry extinguishers" in all circumstances so that worry is utterly obliterated.

Further, angels can help us deal with death—including the death of a pet. According to one strange account I read, an elderly lady had to take her cat to the vet. "Unfortunately, the cat needed to be put to sleep. The lady sat in the waiting room and looked out the window. She saw her cat in the arms of an angel. The angel had the face of a cat and looked at the cat with sheer love and care. Cradling the cat gently, the angel ascended. The lady watched until they were out of sight."[24]

Daniel, Wyllie, and Ramer also allege that angels assist us in helping friends through the gateway of death.

> If you are close to someone who is about to leave the physical plane, you can work with your angel and the guardian of your friend or relation to help that person approach death with more peace of mind, knowing that this is the next step in the journey of evolution. Ask the angels to help you understand the needs of your friend on an empathic level.[25]

These authors explain that "our culture perpetuates the notion that life is short, death is forever, and something to be feared. That isn't the angelic view. They tell us that we are immortal souls, who keep evolving, even after death."[26] We have nothing to fear. All people, regardless of their religious persuasion, go to the "country of the spirit" at death. (This, of course, is utterly contrary to the teachings of Scripture. See, for example, Revelation 20:11-15.)

Angels and a Higher Consciousness

Eileen Freeman, author of *Touched by Angels* (popular among New Agers), believes the angels are among us to help "raise our consciousness."

> The angels are among us to help raise our consciousness, our spiritual awareness as a race, not just as individuals...The whole earth is hovering on the edge of a transformation so glorious that we have no idea how to describe it. The angels are among us as guides,

> to help us through and into a new level of consciousness on earth. And in time, we will come to see the angels who were all around us all the time and live with them as friends and helpers.[27]

Freeman claims that beginning in 1979 and for three years afterward, she received intuitions and "heart-to-heart communications" from her own guardian angel. This angel allegedly informed her that about 250 years ago, many of the angels who are guardians to the human race entered into a new way of working with select human beings. These angels and humans...

> covenanted together to live in a much closer and more obvious spiritual relationship than most humans do, in order to become a leaven among all, for the transformation of the world...
>
> The idea is not that a few privileged become an exclusive club, but that angel and human act as hubs or nuclei around the world, with the aim that in time, all people and their guardian angels will share such close relationships. There's nothing magical or superstitious about it. It's not a private pipeline to God. It's simply another means by which God bestows grace upon us.[28]

Angels as Copilots

Angel enthusiasts tell us that angels are ready and willing to function as copilots of our lives. "If you ever need them to take over, they are ready and capable...Copilots act as your invisible secretaries, arranging and ordering your days so that you don't have to make extra trips, reminding you about appointments and deadlines you are about to miss in your confusion."[29] We can put our lives on "cruise control" with the angels. We should therefore "let go and let the angels." If we do so, the angels will lead us "to a better place" and lighten our loads in life.[30]

Angels and New Religious Experiences

Some angel enthusiasts claim that when a new angelic guide comes into your life, you may develop a desire to learn about a culture or religion that is new to you. You may find yourself purchasing books, artifacts, incense, music, or clothes that will teach you the essence of this new spiritual interest. If, for example, one of your angelic spiritual guides is a Native American, you may find yourself having visions that put you in touch with Mother Earth. You may then end up having a greater respect for the earth.[31]

Michael the archangel is supposedly a strong proponent of free thinking and encourages religious openness and experimentation. "Michael sends us inspiration that urges us to open our minds to new ways of thinking and encourages us to figure out for ourselves where we need to be and how to get there. Creating our own religion can help us free our thinking and figure things out for ourselves. Think about ways the angels can help you form your own religion in a fun and humorous way."[32] (The biblical Michael, in contrast to this New Age impostor, is always doing the bidding of the only true God—see Daniel 10:13-21; 12:1; Jude 9.)

Angels Empower Us

Angels can allegedly empower human beings like nothing else can. Angel enthusiasts urge us to keep in mind that "with God and his angels, nothing…is impossible." Indeed, "with faith, imagination, the angels, and God, you can do anything." We should daily affirm to ourselves, "Whenever I think my mission impossible, the angels venture forward to lead the way."[33]

Custom-Designed Angels

Angel enthusiasts assert that if you need help and you're not sure about what kind of angel might be a benefit to you, all you need to do is to ask that an angel suited to your special need will take over. "A custom-designed angel will arrive and take on the job."[34] For example, if you are a teacher, you can invoke the presence of an angel of education to help you. If you are a student, you can invoke the presence of an angel of study to help you.

Looking Ahead

We have seen some strange ideas about God's heavenly helpers, and we've only touched the tip of the iceberg. We could talk about much more, but space forbids.

In the next chapter, we'll begin learning what Scripture tells us about angels—what they are like and what they do in God's universe. John Calvin, the great Reformer who himself wrote about angels, said, "We should not indulge in speculations concerning the angels, but search out the witness of Scripture."[35] I agree with Calvin wholeheartedly.

The rest of this book assumes that the Bible—God's Word—is the only authoritative source from which we can derive reliable knowledge about angels and other spiritual matters. God created the angels (Colossians 1:16), and He tells us everything we need to know about them.

Celestial Discernment

I would be remiss if I closed chapters 2 through 4—filled with examples of celestial quackery—without providing at least a few points of celestial discernment:[36]

- People who claim they've encountered an angel simply because a stranger showed up unexpectedly, helped them, and then abruptly left may not really have encountered an angel at all. They may have encountered a compassionate human being who left suddenly without saying goodbye.

- People who report seeing an angel upon awakening from sleep may simply have imagined it. The fuzzy state between sleep and full wakefulness is a breeding ground for all kinds of strange experiences.
- Some people who report an angel story may actually be encountering demonic spirits. We must not forget that Satan can masquerade as an "angel of light" (2 Corinthians 11:14). Some of the ideas we've seen are undoubtedly rooted in demonic phenomena.
- Some people who report an angel story may be experiencing a false memory. More and more these days, psychologists are demonstrating just how easily people can develop such false memories. People can even dream something and years later remember it as something that really occurred.
- Some people who make claims about angel phenomena may be lying. Especially if they are seeking to bolster some spiritual or religious point of view, they may choose to fabricate an encounter with a celestial being out of thin air. Nothing bolsters a religious claim like an alleged visitation from the beyond.
- Some people who report an angel story may be exaggerating. People naturally tend to exaggerate and embellish. ("I caught a fish THIS BIG.")

People may think they've encountered an angel because (for example) they think they felt a tap on the shoulder and no humans were present. As they tell their friends about it the next day, they may mention something about a glowing light. Perhaps the day after that they may make reference to a fragrance of flowers that was present.

- We should resist the temptation to reshape angels according to our own fancy instead of basing our knowledge of angels entirely on the teachings of Scripture.
- We should resist the temptation to be overimaginative in interpreting our circumstances. For example, finding a twenty dollar bill in a parking lot, and feeling a sense of peace and serenity as a result, does not mean one has been visited by an angel.[37]

These are times for discernment!

Having made these points, please be assured that I most certainly believe that angels are among us and can even appear among us! But we must be biblical and discerning in our viewpoint. Let's now proceed on an exciting journey through the pages of Scripture and discover the truth about this fascinating celestial doctrine.

PART 2

What Angels Are Like

Praise him, all his angels, praise him, all his heavenly hosts...Let them praise the name of the LORD*, for he commanded and they were created.*

~ Psalm 148:2,5 ~

5

The Origin of Angels

The Bible has a lot to say about angels. The New Testament speaks of them some 175 times; the Old Testament, just over 100 times. Of course, even if the Bible mentioned angels just once, that would be enough for us to accept the doctrine as true. But with hundreds of such references, angelology is obviously an important doctrine for us to understand.[1] This is confirmed in 2 Timothy 3:16, which tells us that "*all* Scripture is God-breathed and is useful for teaching" (emphasis added).

Angels are not confined to just one period of Bible history. Nor are they found in just a few books of the Bible. In fact, angels are mentioned in 34 different Bible books, from the earliest (whether you think Genesis or Job was written first) to the last—the book of Revelation.[2] The existence and activity of angels is prominently displayed all throughout the scriptural witness.

But where did angels come from? Have they been around forever, or did they come into being at a point in time? And if they came into being at a point in time, why, when, and how did that happen? We now turn our attention to these questions.

Let us first be clear, however, that we will find our answers not in the abundant speculations in many of today's angel books but rather in the Bible alone—the only truly reliable and authoritative source on spiritual matters. As the great Reformer John Calvin said, "Wherefore, if we would be duly wise, we must renounce those vain babblings of idle men, concerning the nature, ranks, and number of angels, without any authority from the Word of God."[3] We should certainly not seek to go beyond Scripture, remembering that "the secret things belong to the LORD our God, but the things revealed belong to us and to our children forever" (Deuteronomy 29:29).

Angels Are Created Beings

Some angelologists (people who study the doctrine of angels) have proposed that every new wish or desire that God expresses automatically brings into existence a new angel whose sole mission is to accomplish that wish or desire. They suggest that the lifespan of some of these angels is limited to the duration of their specific duty or service to God. Once they finish their task, they die.[4]

Others believe that humans become angels at the moment of death. This idea has been popularized in a number of movies in recent years.

Both of these ideas are patently unbiblical. As we consult God's Word, one thing becomes abundantly clear: Angels are created beings. They have not existed forever. Nor were they formerly humans. They were created as angels.

In Psalm 148:2-5 we read the following words of worship and praise:

> Praise him, all his angels,
> praise him, all his heavenly hosts.

Praise him, sun and moon,
 praise him, all you shining stars.
Praise him, you highest heavens
 and you waters above the skies.
Let them praise the name of the LORD,
 for he commanded and they were created.

This passage clearly affirms that God spoke the word, and the angels were instantly created. They came into being at a specific point in time.

God's Word also indicates that angels were created as permanent beings; they do not pass out of existence when they complete a particular duty for God. Michael, for example, is pictured as an angelic servant of God in Daniel 12 (hundreds of years before Christ's incarnation) as well as in Revelation 12 (in the end times). Michael, like all other angels, is a permanent spirit being.

The Old Testament consistently portrays God as the Creator. The New Testament, however, explicitly tells us that Jesus Christ was the actual agent of creation. This, of course, is a clear indication of Christ's deity. As God, Christ brought the universe into being (John 1:3; Colossians 1:16; Hebrews 1:2,10; compare with Isaiah 44:24). Let's briefly consider what Scripture tells us about Christ's work as Creator.

John 1:3—Christ Made All Things

John's Gospel tells us, "In the beginning was the Word, and the Word was with God, and the Word was God. He was with God in the beginning. Through him all things were made; without him nothing was made that has been made" (John 1:1-3).

How the apostle John must have exulted as he walked by Jesus' side, knowing that next to him stood the Creator of the universe in all of its vastness! Surely he must have marveled at how the stars above him were the handiwork of his friend, companion, and Savior, Jesus Christ. No wonder John had such a worshipful attitude toward Jesus (John 1:14; 2:11; 20:30-31).

Notice that John states Christ's creative work both positively—"through him all things were made," and negatively—"without him nothing was made that has been made" (John 1:3). John states this truth in both ways because he wanted the reader to fully grasp that Christ Himself is the sovereign Creator of all things, including the entire angelic realm.

How did Christ carry out His creative work? The Scriptures are clear that He merely gave the command, and the universe leapt into existence. Scripture also indicates that when Christ did the work of creation, He did so instantaneously. Psalm 33 tells us, "By the word of the LORD were the heavens made, their starry host by the breath of his mouth...For he spoke, and it came to be; he commanded, and it stood firm" (verses 6,9; compare with Genesis 1:3,6,9,14,20,24).

Hebrews 11:3 likewise tells us that "the universe was formed at God's command." John Whitcomb comments that "it is quite impossible to imagine a time interval in the transition from nonexistence to existence! 'And God said, Let there be light: and there was light' (Genesis 1:3). At one moment there was no light; the next moment there was!"[5] Similarly, at one moment there was no angelic realm; the next moment there was!

The angels apparently were all created simultaneously. As theologian Louis Berkhof puts it, "Their full number was created in the beginning; there has been no increase in their ranks" (see Hebrews 12:22 and Revelation 5:11).[6] Unlike human beings, who are conceived and born at different times in history, all of the angels were created at a single moment. Matthew 22:30 would seem to support this, for there we read that angels do not marry and thus do not have children.[7]

Colossians 1:16—Christ Created the Angels

In keeping with John's testimony, the apostle Paul affirms that by Christ "all things were created: things in heaven and on earth, visible and invisible, whether thrones or powers or rulers or authorities; all things were created by him and for him. He is before all things, and in him all things hold together" (Colossians 1:16-17).

The little phrase "all things" means that Christ created the whole universe of things. "Every form of matter and life owes its origin to the Son of God, no matter in what sphere it may be found, or with what qualities it may be invested...Christ's creative work was no local or limited operation; it was not bounded by this little orb [earth]."[8] Everything—whether it be simple or complex, visible or invisible, heavenly or earthly, immanent or transcendent—is the product of Christ.

Paul says that Christ created "thrones," "powers," "rulers," and "authorities." In the rabbinic (Jewish) thought of the first century, these words described different orders of angels (see Romans 8:38; Ephesians 1:21; 3:10; 6:12; Colossians 2:10,15). Apparently a heresy flourished in Colossae (the city in which the Colossian church was located) that involved the worship of angels and degraded Christ. To correct this grave error, Paul emphasizes in Colossians 1:16 that Christ is the One who created all things—including all the angels—and therefore He is supreme and is alone worthy to be worshipped.[9] As we have seen, to say Christ is the One who created all things is to say Christ is God. John MacArthur makes this clear:

> Both Nehemiah 9:6 ("Thou, even thou, art Lord [Heb. *Yhwh*] alone; thou hast made heaven...with all their host") and Psalm 148:5 ("the Lord [*Yhwh*]...commanded, and they were created") identify *Jehovah* [or

> *Yahweh*] as the One who created the angels. One of the strongest proofs of Jesus' deity is the biblical assertion that He is the One who created all things, including the angels (Colossians 1:16).[10]

The apostle Paul also states of Christ that "all things were created by him and for him" (Colossians 1:16). Creation is "for" Christ in the sense that He is the end for which all things exist. They are meant to serve His will, to contribute to His glory. "Christ is outside creation, prior to it, distinct from it, and He is sovereign over it all, for it was created by Him and indeed for Him."[11]

So angels were created—as were all other things—to serve and glorify Christ, not to act according to their own wills or independently of God. This Christ-centered aspect of angels is almost never mentioned in the current bestselling literature on angels.

When Were the Angels Created?

If angels are created beings, when were they created? More specifically, were they created at the same time as the earth or sometime prior to that? These questions have been consistently debated for centuries.

Saint Augustine commented that Scripture does not plainly state when the angels were created, "but if mention is made, it is implicit under the name of 'heaven,' when it is said, 'In the beginning God created the heavens and the earth.' "[12] In other words, Augustine assumed God created the angels when He created the heavens.

Many theologians through the centuries have suggested that God created the angels sometime prior to the creation of the earth—and we can find good evidence to support this view.

Job 38:7 (KJV), for example, makes reference to the "sons of God" singing at the time the earth was created. Many scholars believe these "sons of God" in Job 38 are angels.[13] Elsewhere in Job, the term *sons of God* refers to angels (Job 1:6; 2:1 KJV). (We will discover why angels are called "sons of God" in chapter 8.)

James Montgomery Boice is representative of contemporary Bible scholars in saying that "if Job 38:7 is to be taken as referring to angels, as there is every reason for it to be, then even before the creation of the material universe [the planets and stars] there was a vast world of spirit beings."[14] These angelic spirit beings sang as a massive choir when God created the earth. What a moment that must have been!

Elect and Evil Angels

All the angels in God's universe were originally created good and holy, just as God made and pronounced all His creation good (Genesis 1:31; 2:3). Jude 6 affirms that originally all the angels were holy creatures. Creating anything wicked—such as evil angels—would be inconsistent with God's holy character.[15] God did not create Lucifer and the fallen angels (demons) in a state of wickedness.

Though God originally created all the angels in a state of holiness, Scripture seems to imply that they were subjected to a period of probation. Some of the angels retained their state of holiness; others did not (see Jude 6 KJV). In other words, some angels remained holy and did not sin, while others—following Lucifer's lead—rebelled against God and fell into great sin.[16] (We will address this angelic rebellion in detail in chapter 15.)

All the angels originally enjoyed God's direct presence (Matthew 18:10; Revelation 12:7-9) and heaven's perfect environment (Mark 13:32). This made the rebellion of some all the more sinful.[17]

Once the angels were put to the test to remain loyal to God or to rebel with Lucifer, their decision seems to have been made permanent. As theologian Charles Ryrie puts it, "Those who successfully passed the probationary test will always stay in that original holy state. Those who failed are now confirmed in their evil, rebellious state."[18]

Good angels are called "elect" angels in 1 Timothy 5:21. They are not elect because they sinned and then were elected unto redemption (they never sinned during the probationary period). Rather, they are elect because God intervened to permanently confirm ("elect") them in their holiness so they could never sin. Louis Berkhof says "they evidently received, in addition to the grace with which all angels were endowed, and which was sufficient to enable them to retain their position, a *special grace of perseverance,* by which they were confirmed in their position."[19] Thus, good angels are now incapable of sinning. The lines have been drawn, and they are now absolute.

Scripture confirms this and indicates that the evil angels who rebelled against God are not redeemable. "Those that followed Satan in his sin fell decisively and are permanently left in their evil state without recourse or even the possibility of redemption. They are irrevocably consigned to the lake of fire (Matthew 25:41)."[20] Theologian Henry Thiessen suggests that "because the angels are a company and not a race, they sinned *individually,* and not in some federal head of the race [as was true with humanity's fall in the person of Adam]. It may be that because of this, God made no provision of salvation for the fallen angels."[21] The evil angels are destined for eternal suffering.

Where Do the Holy Angels Live?

Do angels just live invisibly on earth? Is stellar space their home? Or is their home to be found in the highest heaven, where God Himself dwells?

Though angels apparently have access to the entire universe, God's Word seems to affirm that angels dwell in heaven but are sent out on specific errands or assignments, as was Gabriel in Daniel 9:21 (compare with Mark 13:32).[22] Numerous passages in Scripture speak of heaven, not earth, as the primary home of angels.

- Micaiah refers to "the LORD sitting on his throne with all the host of heaven standing on his right and on his left" (2 Chronicles 18:18). The "host of heaven" refers specifically to the angelic realm.
- Daniel 7:10 describes "thousands upon thousands" of angels attending God in heaven, and "ten thousand times ten thousand" (100 million) angels standing before Him.
- Isaiah 6:1-6 pictures angels hovering around God's throne and proclaiming, "Holy, holy, holy is the LORD Almighty."
- Jesus speaks of angels "ascending and descending" to and from heaven in John 1:51.
- Hebrews 12:22 exhorts believers, "You have come to...the city of the living God. You have come to thousands upon thousands of angels in joyful assembly."
- John the apostle, author of the book of Revelation, said, "I looked and heard the voice of many angels, numbering thousands upon thousands, and ten thousand times ten thousand. They encircled the

> throne and the living creatures and the elders" (Revelation 5:11).

Apparently, then, the natural habitat of angels is in heaven in the very presence of God. When they have an assigned task to perform, they leave the realm of heaven, complete their work on earth (or wherever God sends them), and then return to heaven.

This, of course, is not to discount the possibility that some angels have prolonged assignments on earth. Several Scripture passages clearly show that God has appointed certain angels to guard and protect believers during their earthly sojourns. And what these angels do on behalf of God's children is quite different from what we read about in many of today's bestselling books about angels, as we will soon see.

An angel is a spiritual creature without a body created by God for the service of Christendom and the church.

~ Martin Luther ~

6

The Nature of Angels

Are angels simply figments of our imaginations? Are angels the spirits of people who have died? Are angels personal beings, or are they forces of nature? Are all angels invisible, or do some take on permanent human form? Do all angels have wings? Are there baby angels? How powerful are the angels? How smart are the angels? Can angels act on their own, or must they do only what God tells them to do?

Down through the centuries, people have raised many questions about the nature of angels. Let's see what answers the Bible provides.

Nature or Function

We can begin with the recognition that the term *angel* indicates not the nature of angels but rather their function. The word *angel* simply means "messenger." Angels are God's messengers or ambassadors.[1] Saint Augustine put it this way: "The name Angel refers to their office, not their nature. You ask the name of this nature, it is spirit; you ask its office, it is that of an

Angel, which is a messenger."[2] Keeping this distinction in mind will be helpful throughout the rest of the book.

Were Angels Once People?

Hollywood movies often promote the idea that angels are the spirits of departed human beings. As we noted in the previous chapter, however, Christ Himself created the angels—and He created them *as angels* (Colossians 1:16).

We see the distinction between humans and angels reflected in several biblical passages. For example, Psalm 8:5 indicates that man was made lower than the angels but will be made higher in the afterlife (in heaven). Hebrews 12:22-23 clearly distinguishes the "thousands upon thousands of angels" from the "spirits of righteous men made perfect." First Corinthians 6:3 tells us that in the afterlife, believers will judge or rule over the angels. (This could mean either that angels will be subordinate to redeemed humans in the hereafter or that redeemed humans will participate in judging fallen angels.) As well, 1 Corinthians 13:1 draws a distinction between the tongues (languages) of human beings and of angels.[3] Clearly, the Bible portrays humans and angels as different classes of beings.

Of course, angels and humans do have some similarities. For example, both are created beings, both are finite and limited, both depend on God for their continued existence and well-being, and both are responsible and accountable to God for their actions (see John 16:11; 1 Corinthians 6:3; Hebrews 9:27).[4] But even with those similarities, humans and angels have different natures altogether.

Angels Are Personal Beings

Some people have interpreted all biblical references to angels as metaphoric descriptions of God's work or perhaps as personifications of His power.[5] Such a view clearly goes against the biblical evidence, however.

From a biblical perspective, just as you and I are persons, so also are angels persons (spirit persons) with all the attributes of personality. (Keep in mind that *persons* here means not "people" but simply "beings with a personal nature.") Scripture portrays angels as possessing the personal attributes of intelligence, emotions, and a moral will.

- Intelligence: Angels possess great wisdom (2 Samuel 14:20) and discernment (2 Samuel 14:17), and they use their minds to look into matters (1 Peter 1:12).
- Emotions: Angels are in "joyful assembly" in the presence of God in heaven (Hebrews 12:22). Moreover, they "shouted for joy" at the creation (Job 38:7) and rejoice whenever a sinner repents (Luke 15:7).
- Moral will: Angels make many moral decisions. For example, in Revelation 22:8-9 we see an angel exercise his moral will by forbidding John to worship him and by acknowledging that worship belongs only to God.

Beyond having the attributes of personality, angels perform personal actions. For example, angels love and rejoice (Luke 15:10), they desire (1 Peter 1:12), they contend (Jude 9; Revelation 12:7), they worship (Hebrews 1:6), they talk (Luke 1:13), and they come and go (John 1:51).[6] Clearly, then, angels are persons. As persons, they are able to render personal and intelligent worship to God (Psalm 148:2). They are also held responsible for the quality of their service and their moral choices (see 1 Corinthians 6:3).[7] As well, God sends angels as persons to be ministering spirits (Hebrews 1:14), bringing aid and protection to His people.

Angels Are Incorporeal and Invisible

The Scriptures tell us that angels are incorporeal and invisible. The word *incorporeal* means "lacking material form or substance." Angels are not material, physical beings; they are spirit beings and are therefore invisible. (This doesn't contradict the idea that angels can appear to humans—more on this later.)

Some Jews and early church fathers believed that angels have some kind of airy or fiery bodies. They struggled to understand how a true creature could lack a body.[8] Theologians later concluded that angels are pure spirit beings. They based this view on passages like Hebrews 1:14, where angels are called "ministering spirits."

Because angels do not have physical bodies, they don't get ill, grow old, decay, and eventually die.[9] Angels know nothing of the limitations of having a physical body.[10] God created them as nonphysical beings.

In addition, because angels are invisible, you and I are generally unaware of their activities behind the scenes. We have no way of telling just how many times angels have intervened on our behalf without our being aware of it.

We will soon see that angels, even though they are invisible and incorporeal, can appear visibly to human beings. But normally, angels are not visible to the human eye. You may recall from the Old Testament that the Lord had to open Balaam's eyes before he could see that an angel was standing in his way

(Numbers 22:31). The prophet Elisha had to ask the Lord to open the eyes of his servant; then the young man was able to see a multitude of angelic beings on the mountainside, protecting him and Elisha from their enemies (2 Kings 6:17).

Billy Graham has some great insights on man's inability to see angels.

> While angels may become visible by choice, our eyes are not constructed to see them ordinarily any more than we can see the dimensions of a nuclear field, the structure of atoms, or the electricity that flows through copper wiring. Our ability to sense reality is limited: The deer of the forest far surpass our human capacity in their keenness of smell. Bats possess a phenomenally sensitive built-in radar system. Some animals can see things in the dark that escape our attention. Swallows and geese possess sophisticated guidance systems that appear to border on the supernatural. So why should we think it strange if men fail to perceive the evidences of angelic presence?[11]

God may have chosen to keep humans from being able to perceive angels because of man's tendency to worship and venerate the creation in place of the Creator.[12] Remember what happened to the apostle John? When he was receiving his revelation from the Lord and beheld a mighty angel, his first inclination was to bow down and worship the angel. But the angel instructed John to cease and to render worship only to God (Revelation 22:8-9). Perhaps as a safeguard, then, God purposefully designed man with the inability to perceive His glorious angels.

Angels Are Localized

Even though angels are spirit beings, they seem to have

spatial limitations. They cannot be everywhere at once; Scripture clearly portrays them as having to move from one place to another.

The angel Gabriel engaged in "swift flight" to travel from heaven to Daniel's side (Daniel 9:21-23). Then, in Daniel 10:10-14, we read about a different angel who was delayed on his errand by another spirit being—apparently a demon. One Bible scholar made this observation about the delay: "Here a time limitation corresponds with spatial limitation. If a time lapse is involved in their changing locations, this means they are localized."[13]

After a group of angels appeared visibly to some shepherds in a field to announce the birth of Christ, the angels left them and went back into heaven (Luke 2:15). Angels can only be in one place at a time and must engage in spatial travel to go from one place to another. Christ Himself spoke of angels ascending and descending from heaven (John 1:51).

Do All Angels Have Wings?

Angels are commonly depicted on postcards, cartoons, magazines, and other literature as having wings. But do all angels have wings?

Scripture makes it clear to us that many angels have wings. For example, the seraphim described in Isaiah 6:1-5 have wings, as do the cherubim Ezekiel saw in his vision (Ezekiel 1:6) and the angels the apostle John saw in his vision (Revelation 4:8). But many other Bible verses about angels don't mention wings (for example, Hebrews 13:2). What can we conclude from this?

All of God's angels might have wings, but this is not a necessary inference. Theologian Millard Erickson explains that "the cherubim and seraphim are represented as winged (Exodus 25:20; Isaiah 6:2)...However, we have no assurance that what is true of cherubim and seraphim is true of angels in general. Since there is no explicit reference indicating that angels *as a whole* are winged, we must regard this as at best an inference, but not a necessary inference, from the biblical passages which describe them as flying."[14]

Some people have suggested that the wings of angels are symbolic and may not actually be necessary for flight. "The wings pictured in angelic visions (note they do not always appear with wings) may be symbols of their swiftness to execute God's wishes, just as wind and fire symbolize their fast and fervent service (Hebrews 1:7)."[15]

For angels to have wings does not contradict what we learned earlier about angels as spirit beings who are by nature invisible and incorporeal (Hebrews 1:14). Winged angels are spirit beings who are nonphysical and are naturally invisible to the human eye.

Angels Can Appear as Men

Though angels are normally invisible, they can nevertheless appear as men (Matthew 1:20; Luke 1:26; John 20:12).[16] Their resemblance to men can be so realistic, in fact, that they are actually taken to be human beings (Hebrews 13:2).

Recall from the Old Testament that Abraham welcomed three "men" in the plains of Mamre (Genesis 18:1-8). These "men" walked, talked, sat down, and ate—just like normal men—but they were not men; they were angels (see Genesis 18:22; 19:1). Now, we have no scriptural evidence that angels need food for sustenance. But apparently they can appear as men and eat like men during the course of fulfilling their assigned task in the realm of humanity. [17]

So a person who helped you during a time of need could have been an angel who appeared as a human. We have no reason to believe that such appearances cannot occur today just as they did in biblical times.

Some people have wondered if the Bible includes any examples of an angel appearing in a female form. The answer is no. In reality, of course, angels are genderless beings. So why do angels typically appear as men? Peter Kreeft suggests that "the function of angels among men is to be God's messengers and God's warriors—two jobs that in nearly all societies, times, and places males rather than females perform."[18] For angels to appear among humans as men makes good sense.

Some have raised the possibility that Hebrews 13:2 may allow for the possibility of an angel appearing as a woman: "Do not forget to entertain strangers, for by so doing some people have entertained angels without knowing it." They suggest that nothing in the context of Hebrews 13:2 limits "strangers" to male strangers.

In the Bible, angels have also appeared in a variety of nonhuman-like ways. Herbert Lockyer makes this note:

> On occasion angels appear to humanity in various natural forms. In the famous call of Moses to liberate the Israelites from bondage in Egypt, in Exodus 3:2, an angel speaks to Moses in the form of a burning bush (see also Acts 7:30,35). Again, the angel of the Lord conducted the Israelites through the wilderness by means of a cloud (Exodus 14:19). Angels can also make their appearance in dreams, as to Joseph prior to the birth of Jesus (Matthew 1:20,24; 2:13,19), and in visions, as to Cornelius, the centurion (Acts 10:3).[19]

We should not expect angels to appear in dreams, visions, clouds, and bushes in our day. Theologians generally categorize the angel appearances in the paragraph above as descriptive, not prescriptive. That is, these Bible verses describe how some angels appeared in Bible times in the outworking of God's redemptive plan for humanity. They do not prescribe what Christians should expect to see in every century since that time.

Angels Are Powerful

The Scriptures portray angels as extremely powerful and mighty beings. Indeed, Psalm 103:20 calls them "mighty ones who do his bidding." Second Thessalonians 1:7 refers to God's "powerful angels."

We see an example of angelic strength in Matthew 28, where we read that an angel rolled away the giant stone at the sepulcher of Jesus (verses 2-7). Some people have estimated that a wheel of granite like the one that guarded the tomb—about eight feet in diameter and one foot thick—would weigh more than four tons (8000 pounds).[20] Yet an angel flipped the stone out of the way as if it were a mere pebble.

In Scripture, some angels seem to be more powerful than others. As noted earlier, Daniel 10:13 tells us that an angel who had been sent by God to accomplish a task was detained by a more powerful fallen angel (a demon). Only when the archangel Michael showed up to render aid was the lesser angel freed to carry out his task.

Angels Are Not Omnipotent

Even though angels have great power, none of them (including the archangel Michael) are omnipotent (all-powerful) like God. Angels are creatures with creaturely limitations.

This is important to observe because angels are no replacement for God—as some angel enthusiasts seem to imply in their writings. Angels derive power from and depend on God. And they always exercise their power on behalf of God, never to achieve their own ends.

Angels Are Holy

We noted in the previous chapter that angels who passed their probationary test and did not sin were confirmed in their holiness (see 1 Timothy 5:21). But what does it mean to be holy?

The word *holy* comes from a root word that means "set apart." God's angels are set apart from sin and set apart to God to serve Him and carry out His assigned tasks.

Scripture often refers to angels simply as God's "holy ones" (Job 5:1; 15:15; Psalm 89:7; Daniel 4:13,17,23; 8:13; Jude 14). They are set apart to God in every way. Their commitment to Him is complete. They find joy in pleasing their Creator.

All this is in marked contrast to the fallen angels—demons—who are unholy in every way. They are set apart from righteousness and set apart to the devil to do his unholy bidding. They are against everything related to God. As we will see later on, however, their time is limited, and their ultimate destiny is the lake of fire.

Angels Are Obedient

God's "holy ones" are obedient to Him. Their obedience to their Creator reflects their holiness. In Psalm 103:20, the psalmist exults, "Praise the LORD, you his angels, you mighty ones who do his bidding, who obey his word." As Bible expositor Albert Barnes put it, the angels "are prompt to do His will, rapid, quick, and obedient in His service."[21]

As we noted earlier, angels do not interact among humans to do their own bidding. Rather, they act under instruction from God. The only reason angels minister to believers during their earthly sojourns is because God has ordained them to.

Matthew 6:10 also speaks of the obedience of God's holy angels. In this part of the Lord's Prayer we find the words, "Your kingdom come, your will be done on earth as it is in heaven." On the surface, this may seem an unlikely verse in support of the obedience of angels. But many scholars believe Matthew 6:10 is saying, "May God's will be done among humans on earth as it is already being done by the holy angels in heaven." If this interpretation is correct, the angels exemplify unwavering obedience to God.

Angels Have Great Knowledge

Though angels are not omniscient (all-knowing) like God, they do possess great wisdom and intelligence. They were created as a higher order of creatures than humans (see Psalm 8:5). Therefore, they innately possess a greater knowledge than man.

Beyond this, angels gain ever-increasing knowledge through long observation of human activities. Unlike people, angels do not have to study the past; they have experienced it. They have witnessed firsthand how other people have acted and reacted in certain situations and thus can accurately predict how we may act in similar circumstances. The experiences of longevity give angels greater knowledge.[22]

Angels Are Immortal

Angels live forever. Once created, they never cease to exist. Indeed, Scripture clearly states that angels are not subject to death (Luke 20:36).[23]

In Daniel 9, the angel Gabriel appeared to the prophet Daniel. Then, more than 500 years later, this same unaged Gabriel appeared to Zechariah, the father of John the Baptist (Luke 1).[24]

Since angels are immortal and do not die—and since they do not propagate baby angels (Matthew 22:30)—the number of angels is and always will be the same.[25]

Bringing the Facts Together

In our brief survey we have discovered a number of fascinating insights about the nature of angels:

- Angels are not departed human beings. When God created angels, He created them as angels.
- Angels are personal beings with all the attributes of personality—mind, emotions, and will.
- Angels are incorporeal (lacking material substance) and invisible.
- Though angels are invisible, they can appear to humans.
- Angels are localized and have to engage in spatial travel to go from one place to another.
- Some (possibly even all) angels have wings.
- Angels have great power, though they are not omnipotent (all-powerful).
- Angels are holy (they are set apart from sin and set apart to God).
- Angels are obedient to God.
- Angels possess greater intelligence than humans though they are not omniscient (all-knowing) like God.
- Angels are immortal—they do not die.

And that is just the beginning of what the Bible tells us about angels!

That the universe should be ordered around a series of over/under hierarchical relationships is God's idea, a part of His original design.

~ Duane Litfin ~

7

The Organization of Angels

There has been much speculation regarding just how many angels there are. The great logician Thomas Aquinas believed there are many times more angels than there are human beings. Saint Albert the Great calculated that there were exactly 399,920,004 angels. The Kabbalists of medieval Judaism determined there were precisely 301,655,722 angels.[1]

Clement of Alexandria in the second century AD suggested that there are as many angels as there are stars in the stellar heavens.[2] This is based on the idea that angels are associated with the stars in Scripture (Job 38:7; Psalm 148:1-3; Revelation 9:1-2; 12:3-4,7-9). If Clement is correct, the number of angels would exceed the stars visible to the human eye—approximately 6000 during a year. Scientists say the total number of stars in the universe may run into the billions.[3]

Theologian Charles Ryrie says that "some have suggested that there are as many angels in the universe as the total number of all human beings throughout history."[4] He further suggests this may be implied in the words of Jesus recorded in Matthew

18:10: "See that you do not look down on one of these little ones. For I tell you that their angels in heaven always see the face of my Father in heaven." Some people reason that this could be interpreted to mean that every child who has ever lived has had an angelic counterpart in heaven.

Peter Kreeft suggests that the angels must outnumber the human beings alive at any one time: "How many angels are there? More than five billion, for everyone has a guardian angel…There must be many more angels than humans." Kreeft thus suggests, "There are twice as many persons as we can see in every place, every kitchen, or classroom, every hospital or nursery. Only half are *human* persons."[5]

The Scriptures indicate that the number of angels is vast indeed. We find reference to "a great company of the heavenly host" (Luke 2:13), and the angels are spoken of as "tens of thousands and thousands of thousands" (Psalm 68:17; see also Daniel 7:10). Their number is elsewhere described as "myriads of myriads" (Revelation 5:11 NASB).

Daniel 7:10, speaking of God, says that "thousands upon thousands [of angels] attended him; ten thousand times ten thousand stood before him." The number "ten thousand times ten thousand" is 100 million. This is a number almost too vast to fathom. Job 25:3 understandably asks, "Can his forces be numbered?"

Scripture never specifies the precise number of angels in the universe, but two things are certain:

1. However many angels there are, their number certainly never increases or decreases. We have noted earlier that angels do not die, nor do they propagate and give birth to baby angels. The number of angels remains perfectly constant at all times.[6]

2. The angels are not innumerable to God, for He knows each one. As David Jeremiah put it, "The Scriptures say He's counted the hairs on our head (Matthew 10:30). And He's numbered and named all the stars (Psalm 147:4) and knows that 'not one of them is missing' (Isaiah 40:26). If He's calculated totals for the stars and our hair, He surely has the angels tallied."[7]

Ranks in the Angelic Realm

The angels of God are not only numerous but also well organized. Our God is a God of order, and the angelic realm reflects this characteristic. Angels of different ranks and power individually and collectively serve God in the outworking of His sovereign will. Let's note what Scripture says about their varying ranks.

- In Colossians 1:16 we read, "By [Christ] all things were created: things in heaven and on earth, visible and invisible, whether thrones or powers or rulers or authorities; all things were created by him and for him."[8]
- Colossians 2:10 says Christ "is the head over every power and authority."
- In 1 Peter 3:22 we read that Christ "has gone into heaven and is at God's right hand—with angels, authorities and powers in submission to him."
- Ephesians 1:20-21 describes Christ's authority as "far above all rule and authority, power and dominion, and every title that can be given, not only in the present age but also in the one to come."

What do the terms *rulers, principalities, powers, thrones,* and *dominions* mean in these and other such verses? In the rabbinic (Jewish) thought of the first century, these words were used to describe the hierarchical organization in the angelic realm. Reformed scholar Louis Berkhof says, "These appellations do not point to different kinds of angels, but simply to differences of rank or dignity among them."[9]

It is difficult to say for sure what the specific terms mean in reference to the various ranks of angels. But theologians have suggested some likely interpretations.

"Thrones" may be angelic beings in the immediate presence of God—in the immediate vicinity of His glorious throne.[10] They may even sit on their own lesser thrones, pointing to their derived authority under the greater authority of God. These beings may be invested with regal power by which they carry out the sovereign bidding of God. Clement of Alexandria, an early church father, offered an alternate view, suggesting that "thrones" were so called because they either formed or supported the throne of Almighty God.[11]

The "dominions" are apparently next in dignity to the "thrones."[12] These angels exercise dominion over specific domains in carrying out the sovereign bidding of God.

"Rulers" are next in line and exercise rule as assigned by God. We are not told what their rule consists of. But like the other angels in authority, the ruler angels reflect the fact that God is characterized by order and organization in the way He governs the universe.

"Authorities" are possibly subordinates who serve under one of the other orders of angels.[13] Again, we are not told any specifics, but these angelic beings clearly carry out imperial responsibility.[14]

Renowned Bible expositor Joseph Lightfoot makes the

important point that the combination of the words *rulers* and *authorities* are applied "not only to good angels but to bad, not only to spiritual powers but to earthly."[15] Just as humans are in authority over other humans, so also holy angels are in authority over other holy angels, and fallen angels are in authority over other fallen angels.

Beyond these specific angelic ranks, Scripture also speaks of other angels who have varying levels of authority and dignity—including the archangel Michael, the cherubim, the seraphim, and Gabriel. Let's briefly consider each of these.

Michael the Archangel

The word *archangel* implies a rank first among angels. Apparently Michael is in authority over all the other angels—including the thrones, dominions, rulers, and authorities. The term *archangel* occurs just twice in the New Testament, and in both instances it is singular and is preceded by the definite article *the* ("the archangel"—1 Thessalonians 4:16; Jude 9). Some scholars conclude from this that the term is restricted to a single archangel—Michael.[16]

Charles Ryrie, for example, says, "Only Michael is designated as the archangel or high-ranking angel (Jude 9; 1 Thessalonians 4:16). Nowhere does the Bible speak of archangels [plural], though there evidently are other high-ranking angels (Daniel 10:13), yet only one archangel. When Paul says that the voice of the archangel will be heard at the [rapture] of the church, he does not seem to feel the need to name that archangel, which supports the conclusion that there is only one."[17]

Other scholars, however, say that "the definite article with archangel does not necessarily limit the class of archangel to Michael. The article may be one of identification as the *well-known* archangel instead of limitation as the *only* archangel.

There may be others of the same class or rank, since he is described as 'one of the chief princes' (Daniel 10:13)."[18] Jewish tradition has always held that there are seven archangels.[19]

Regardless of whether there is one or more than one archangel, Michael is undeniably the prominent archangel. He is called a chief prince (Daniel 10:13) and "the great prince" (Daniel 12:1), and he seems to lead the other angels (Revelation 12:7). Bible scholar Clinton Arnold tells us that the word *prince* is a title of authority and, when used of angels, refers to beings in authority over a host of angels in battle. Michael, as a chief prince and great prince (and especially as the archangel) would be in authority over all the "prince angels."[20]

Michael appears to be specially related to Israel as her guardian (Daniel 12:1). Louis Berkhof says of Michael, "We see in him the valiant warrior fighting the battles of Jehovah against the enemies of Israel and against the evil powers in the spirit-world."[21] Tony Evans makes a similar comment:

> According to Daniel 12:1, the archangel Michael is the special guardian and protector of Israel, which helps to explain why Israel has been victorious time and again over vastly superior forces in the nation's struggle for existence. The reason Israel will never be wiped off the map is that it's not just about who is fighting on earth. It's also about an archangel whom God has charged with making sure no one destroys His chosen people.[22]

Michael's name means "Who is like God?"[23] His name humbly points to the incomparability of God. It speaks of Michael's complete and unwavering devotedness to God, which stands in stark contrast with Satan, who in his pride declared, "I will be like the most High" (Isaiah 14:14 KJV).[24]

A controversial question that comes up from time to time relates to the claim that appearances of Michael in the Bible were actually appearances of Jesus Christ, the second person of the triune Godhead. Is this a possibility, or does Scripture forbid such an interpretation? I believe at least five biblical arguments make such an interpretation impossible.

1. The archangel Michael does not have the authority in himself to rebuke Satan. Jude 9 tells us, "But Michael the archangel, when he disputed with the devil and argued about the body of Moses, did not dare pronounce against him a railing judgment, but said, 'The Lord rebuke you'" (NASB). By contrast, Jesus rebuked the devil on a number of different occasions (see, for example, Matthew 4:10; 16:23). Since Michael could not rebuke the devil in his own authority and Jesus could (and did) rebuke the devil in His own authority, Michael and Jesus cannot be the same person.

Notice that Michael the archangel said, "The Lord rebuke you." The Greek word for "Lord" in this verse is *kurios*. It is the standard word for *Lord* in the New Testament. It is also a direct parallel to the word *Yahweh* or *Jehovah* in the Old Testament. Jesus is called *kurios* many times in the New Testament, but Michael is never called *kurios*.

For example, we are told that Jesus is *kurios* in Philippians 2:9-11 and that at the name of Jesus every knee will bow in heaven and on earth and under the earth, and every tongue will confess that Jesus is Lord. The apostle Paul, an Old Testament scholar par excellence, is here alluding to Isaiah 45:22-24: "I am God, and there is no other. By myself I have sworn, my mouth has uttered in all integrity a word that will not be revoked: Before me every knee will bow; by me every tongue will swear." Paul was drawing on his vast knowledge of the Old Testament to make the point that Jesus Christ is *kurios* and *Yahweh*—the Lord of all humankind.

The point is this: When Michael said, "The Lord rebuke you," he was appealing directly to the sovereign authority of the Lord of the universe. And Jesus is clearly the sovereign Lord of the universe.

2. Daniel 10:13 calls Michael "one of the chief princes." Whether or not other archangels exist, the fact that Michael is "one of" the chief princes indicates that he is one among a group of chief princes. How large that group is, we are not told. But the scriptural statement that Michael is one in a group proves that he is not utterly unique. By contrast, the Greek word used to describe Jesus in John 3:16 is *monogenes*—which means "unique" or "one of a kind."

The Bible never calls Jesus a chief prince. In fact, He is called the "King of kings and Lord of lords" in Revelation 19:16. This title indicates absolute sovereignty and authority. A King of kings and Lord of lords is much higher in authority than a mere chief prince (who is one in a group of princes). The former has absolute sovereignty and authority; the latter has derived, limited authority.

3. Hebrews 1:5 tells us God never addressed an angel as His son. Since Jesus is the Son of God, and since God never calls an angel His son, Jesus cannot possibly be the archangel Michael.

4. Hebrews 1:6 tells us that the angels worship Christ. This is the exact same word (Greek: *proskuneo*) used of worshipping Jehovah God in the Bible. Christ is worshipped with the same kind of worship rendered to the Father (Revelation 4:10-11; 5:11-12). No one can get around this fact. Jesus is not an angel; the angels worship Him.

Commentator Ray Stedman notes that in the Old Testament, "the angels are called to worship Yahweh (Jehovah). New Testament writers apply such passages without hesitation to Jesus.

Many places in Scripture witness the obedience of the angels, notably Job 38:7, Luke 2:13, and Revelation 5:11-12. Mark 3:11 indicates that even the demons (fallen angels) fell down before Jesus when they saw him and addressed him as the Son of God."[25]

5. Hebrews 2:5 says that the world is not (and never will be) subject to an angel. Certain angels—such as the archangel Michael, principalities, powers, dominions, and thrones—have various ranks and, under God, exercise imperial authority in different ways. But no angel rules the world or God's kingdom.

The backdrop to Hebrews 2:5 is that the Dead Sea Scrolls (discovered at Qumran in 1947) reflect an expectation that the archangel Michael would be a supreme figure in the coming messianic kingdom. It may be that some of the recipients of the book of Hebrews were tempted to assign angels a place above Christ. Whether or not this is so, Hebrews 2:5 clearly teaches that no angel (Michael included) will rule God's kingdom.

If no angel can rule the world (Hebrews 2:5), then Christ cannot be the archangel Michael because over and over again Scripture names Christ as the ruler of God's kingdom (for example, Genesis 49:10; 2 Samuel 7:16; Psalm 2:6; Daniel 7:13-14; Matthew 2:1-2; Luke 1:32-33; Revelation 19:16).

None of this denigrates Michael in any way, but it draws the very important distinction between Christ as the eternal Creator-God and Michael as the created archangel. Michael is a creature with creaturely limitations. And he exists to carry out Christ's sovereign bidding.

The Cherubim: Angels of Power and Majesty

Scripture depicts the cherubim as powerful and majestic angelic creatures who surround God's throne and defend His holiness from any contamination by sin (Genesis 3:24; Exodus

25:18,20; Ezekiel 1:1-18).[26] They are indescribably beautiful and powerful spirit-beings of the highest order (Ezekiel 1:5-14; 28:12-14,17).

Ezekiel 1 speaks of four living creatures in the midst of a burning fire. Later on, they are explicitly identified as cherubim (Ezekiel 10:1). Expositor Charles Dyer summarizes Ezekiel's description of the cherubim this way:

> The general appearance of the living beings was somewhat like a man. However, they would not be mistaken for humans.
>
> They each had four faces and four wings...The cherubim's legs were straight, which implies that they were standing upright, but their feet were calf-like instead of human, and were like burnished (highly polished) bronze. Ezekiel said the four cherubim also had human-like hands...Having four faces on four sides of their heads and being connected in a square, they were able to travel straight in any direction and to change direction without turning.[27]

The cherubim—obviously very high-ranking angels—guard Eden after the expulsion of Adam and Eve (Genesis 3:24). Figures of cherubim adorned the ark of the covenant and were positioned in such a way that they gazed on the mercy seat (Exodus 25:17-20). Cherubim also adorned Solomon's temple (1 Kings 6:23-35). They were represented on the veil that barred the entrance to the Holy of Holies.[28] As well, cherubim are portrayed in the Old Testament as the chariot on which God descends to the earth (2 Samuel 22:11; Psalm 18:10).

The etymology of the word *cherubim* is not known for certain, though some have suggested that the word means "to guard." Certainly this meaning would fit well with their function of guarding the entrance of Eden (Genesis 3:24). This meaning also fits with the cherubim on the temple veil that barred entrance into the Holy of Holies (Exodus 26:31; 2 Chronicles 3:14). The cherubim are apparently guardians of God's holiness.

Scripture portrays the cherubim as angels even though they are never actually called angels. This may be because they do not function as messengers in their duties. (Remember, the word *angel* literally means "messenger.") We never see the cherubim bringing revelation or instruction from God to men.[29]

The Seraphim: God's "Burning Ones"

We encounter seraphim only in Isaiah's vision recorded in Isaiah 6.

> In the year that King Uzziah died, I saw the Lord seated on a throne, high and exalted, and the train of his robe filled the temple.
>
> Above him were seraphs, each with six wings: With two wings they covered their faces, with two they covered their feet, and with two they were flying.
>
> And they were calling to one another: "Holy, holy, holy is the LORD Almighty; the whole earth is full of his glory."
>
> At the sound of their voices the doorposts and thresholds shook and the temple was filled with smoke.
>
> "Woe to me!" I cried. "I am ruined! For I am a man of unclean lips, and I live among a people of unclean lips, and my eyes have seen the King, the LORD Almighty."
>
> Then one of the seraphs flew to me with a live coal in his hand, which he had taken with tongs from the altar.

> With it he touched my mouth and said, "See, this has touched your lips; your guilt is taken away and your sin atoned for" (Isaiah 6:1-7).

The Hebrew term *seraphim* literally means "burning ones."[30] This no doubt speaks of their consuming devotion to serving God. "They are afire with adoration of the holy God. Their great cry is in praise of the perfect holiness of God. To ascribe the term 'holy' to God three times means, according to Hebrew idiom, to recognize God as extremely, perfectly holy. Therefore, they *praise and proclaim the perfect holiness of God.*"[31]

The wings of the seraphim may be loaded with symbolic meaning: The fact that two wings cover their faces seems to communicate that even the holy angels cannot look upon the full, unveiled glory of God. (First Timothy 6:16 tells us that God dwells in "unapproachable light.") Some suggest that the seraphim cover their eyes in order to exercise care "not to pry into God's secrets and counsels."[32] That two wings cover their feet apparently symbolizes their reverence. With their third pair of wings the seraphim fly—swiftly carrying out commands they receive from God on the throne.[33]

Gabriel: Mighty One of God

The name *Gabriel* literally means "mighty one of God." The name speaks of the incredible power God gave him. He is distinguished as an angel who stands in the very presence of God (Luke 1:19), evidently in some preeminent sense.[34] His high rank in the angelic realm is obvious from both his name and his continuous standing in God's presence. When carrying out God's bidding, Gabriel can apparently fly swiftly—perhaps faster than most of the other angels (Daniel 9:21).

In Scripture, Gabriel brings revelation to the people of

God—often prophetic in revelation—regarding God's purpose and program.[35] As Herbert Lockyer put it, Gabriel is "an interpreter of the prophetic Word" and "a revealer of the purposes of God."[36] For example, in the Old Testament he appeared to the prophet Daniel (Daniel 8:16; 9:21). Gabriel revealed the future by interpreting a vision for Daniel (8:17) and gave understanding and wisdom to him (9:22).[37] In the New Testament (some 500 years later), Gabriel brought the message to Zechariah about the birth of John the Baptist and announced the birth of Jesus to the Virgin Mary (Luke 1:11-17,26-38).[38]

Some people may be tempted to think that Gabriel's responsibility of bringing revelation to human beings is a lowly one unbefitting to one of heaven's greatest angels. This is not the case, however. God entrusted to Gabriel alone the greatest messages that ever left the courts of heaven—including the message of Christ's approaching birth. In choosing Gabriel for such tasks, God honored the great angel before the entire angelic realm.[39]

God's Ordered Universe

The biblical worldview rests on the assumption that a personal God sovereignly designed an ordered universe to function in a particular way. Crucial to this worldview is the concept of authority. Romans 13:1 tells us that God is the source of all authority and even the very concept of authority. "That the universe should be ordered around a series of over/under hierarchical relationships is His idea, a part of His original design. He delegates His authority according to His own pleasure to those whom He places in appropriate positions and it is to Him that His creatures submit when they acknowledge that authority."[40]

God has set up authority structures in the church (1 Timothy 2:11-15; 1 Corinthians 11:2-16; 14:33-36), in the family unit (1 Corinthians 11:3; Ephesians 5:22-23), and in the angelic realm (Ephesians 1:20-21; Colossians 1:16; 2:10; 1 Peter 3:22). And all of these lesser authorities are in submission to the great authority of Christ Himself (Colossians 2:10).

As Christians, we should take great comfort in how God has set up His universe. For He has ordained various authority structures—including that of the entire angelic realm—for the optimum benefit of His creatures and for the outworking of His sovereign will in the universe.

For the ancients a name is not simply a conventional designation, but rather an expression of a being's place in the universe.

~ Henri Cazelles ~

8

The Titles of Angels

In the ancient world a name or title was not a mere label as it is today. Rather, a name or title was a statement that revealed something about the person bearing it. We learn something about a person's nature and function by studying his or her name or title.

As we read the Scriptures, we see that the angels' various titles reveal a great deal about them. In the Bible we find that angels are called sons of God, ministering spirits, God's heavenly host, holy ones, and watchers, among various other titles. Let's examine these representative titles and learn more about angels' nature and function.

Angels as Sons of God

Earlier we noted that the Bible sometimes refers to angels as "sons of God" (for example, Job 1:6; 2:1; 38:7 KJV). What does this title mean in reference to angels? And how does it differ from Jesus' designation as the Son of God?

The words *son of* can carry different meanings in different contexts. A look at any Greek lexicon makes this abundantly clear. The term can be used in one way in regard to angels and quite another way when used of the person of Jesus Christ.

Theologians are virtually unanimous in saying that angels are sons of God in the sense of being created directly by the hand of God.[1] The phrase *sons of God*, when used of angels, simply denotes spirit beings who were brought into existence by a direct creative act of God.[2] Every angel that exists was a direct creation of God.

Remember also that angels do not give birth to other angels (Matthew 22:30). We never read of "sons of angels." Since every single angel was directly created by the hand of God, the name *sons of God* is appropriate.

If the phrase *sons of God* in Genesis 6:2-4 is a reference to fallen angels, as many Bible expositors believe, then even fallen angels are sons of God in the sense that He created them. Of course, they were not created as fallen angels. These angels rebelled against God some time after their creation and became fallen.

How does all this relate to Christ being called the Son of God? This is an important question, for Christ is not in the same league as the angels (though some cultists try to argue that He is). A person will go far astray unless he or she sees a clear distinction between Christ as the Son of God and angels as sons of God. As we will see, the Bible indicates that Christ is eternally the Son of God. How do we know this? Consider the following.

To begin, a word study of the phrase *son of* indicates that it can mean "of the order of" in certain contexts.[3] The phrase is often used this way in the Old Testament. For example, *sons of the prophets* meant "of the order of prophets" (1 Kings 20:35). *Sons of the singers* meant "of the order of singers" (Nehemiah 12:28 KJV). Likewise, the phrase *Son of God,* used of Christ, means "of the order of God" and represents a claim to undiminished deity.

Ancient Eastern people sometimes used the phrase *son of* to indicate likeness or sameness of nature and equality of being.[4] When Jesus claimed to be the Son of God, His Jewish contemporaries fully understood that He was using the term in this way—making a claim to be God in an unqualified sense. Benjamin Warfield affirms that from the earliest days of Christianity, the phrase *Son of God*—when used of Jesus Christ—was understood to be fully equivalent to *God.*[5]

This is why, when Jesus claimed to be the Son of God, the Jews tried to kill Him: "For this reason the Jews tried all the harder to kill him; not only was he breaking the Sabbath, but he was even calling God his own Father, making himself equal with God" (John 5:18). The Jews later said, "We have a law, and according to that law he must die, because he claimed to be the Son of God" (John 19:7). The Jews recognized that Jesus was identifying Himself as God, and they wanted to put Him to death for what they thought was blasphemy (see Leviticus 24:16).

We find clear evidence for Christ's eternal sonship in God's Word. For example, He was already the Son of God before His human birth in Bethlehem. Recall Jesus' discussion with Nicodemus in John 3, when He said, "God so loved the world that he gave his one and only Son, that whoever believes in him shall not perish but have eternal life. For God did not send his Son into the world to condemn the world, but to save the world through him" (John 3:16-17). That Christ, as the Son of God, was sent into the world implies that He was the Son before the incarnation.

Related to this, chapter 30 in the book of Proverbs was

written by a godly man named Agur. In the first four verses, Agur reflects on man's inability to comprehend the infinite God. Because of this inability, he abases himself and humbly acknowledges his ignorance. He effectively communicates the idea that reverence of God is the beginning of true wisdom.

In verse 4, Agur couches his reflections in a series of questions:

> Who has gone up to heaven and come down? Who has gathered up the wind in the hollow of his hands?
>
> Who has wrapped up the waters in his cloak? Who has established all the ends of the earth?
>
> What is his name, and the name of his son? Tell me if you know!

Many scholars—including renowned Old Testament scholars F. Delitzsch and A.R. Fausset—concede that this verse is likely an Old Testament reference to the first and second persons of the Trinity, the eternal Father and the eternal Son of God.[6] This portion of Scripture is not predictive prophecy—it is not speaking about a future Son of God. Rather, it speaks of God the Father and God the Son in present-tense terms during Old Testament times.

Obviously, the answer to each of the four questions in Proverbs 30:4 must be *God*. And the very fact that Agur asked about the name of God's Son seems to imply a recognition, by divine inspiration, of plurality within the Godhead.[7]

We find further evidence for Christ's eternal sonship in Hebrews 1:2, which says God created the universe through His Son—implying that Christ was the Son of God prior to the creation. Moreover, Christ as the Son existed before all things (Colossians 1:17; compare with verses 13-14). As well, Jesus, speaking as the Son of God (John 8:54-56), asserts His eternal preexistence before Abraham (verse 58).

Clearly then, Scripture affirms that Jesus is eternally the Son of God. To relegate Christ to a position less than God simply because of His title *Son of God* is to woefully misunderstand what the term really meant among the ancients.

In contrast, angels, as sons of God, are created beings. In fact, Scripture tells us that the angels were created by Jesus Christ, the Son of God (Colossians 1:16; John 1:3; Hebrews 1:2,10). This in itself sets a wide chasm between Christ and the angels. After all, the same Bible that tells us Christ created the angels also tells us that only God can be the Creator (Isaiah 44:24).

Angels as Ministering Spirits

Hebrews 1:14 asks, "Are not all angels ministering spirits sent to serve those who will inherit salvation?" This brief statement about angels is packed with meaning.

The word *ministering* comes from a Greek word that means "to serve." Angels are spirit-servants who render aid to believers in the outworking of God's purpose on earth. And notice that the author of Hebrews says all angels fall into this category. "Even the most exalted angel is employed in the comparatively humble office of a ministering spirit appointed to assist the heirs of salvation."[8]

What form does this service take? Popular author Ray Stedman says "such ministry involves protection (Psalm 91:11), guidance (Genesis 19:16-17), encouragement (Judges 6:12), deliverance (Acts 12:7), supply (Psalm 105:40), enlightenment (Matthew 2:19-20), and empowerment (Luke 22:43)." Stedman also notes that "their service is rendered largely unseen and often unrecognized, but a passage like [Hebrews 1:14] should make us watchful for such help and grateful to the gracious Lord who sends angels to our aid."[9]

Notice that Hebrews 1:14 tells us that angels are *sent* to render service to the heirs of salvation. God specifically appoints angels to carry out tasks on behalf of believers. They are all under His control and are subordinate to Him. This is important to keep in mind, for many angel enthusiasts today have focused so much attention on angels that they leave God almost entirely out of the picture. We must never forget that angels assist us because God has ordained them to.

Commenting on Hebrews 1:14, expositor Albert Barnes says that "it is a great principle of the divine administration that one class of God's creatures are to minister to others; that one is to aid another—to assist him in trouble, to provide for him when poor, and to counsel him in perplexity." Barnes keenly points out, "As man was ruined in the fall by the temptation offered by one of an angelic, though fallen nature [Satan], why should not others of angelic, unfallen holiness come to assist in repairing the evils which their fallen, guilty brethren have inflicted on the race?"[10]

Within God's sovereign plan, then, the angels assist human beings. This amounts to the strong aiding the weak, the enlightened aiding the ignorant, the pure aiding the impure, and the unfallen aiding the fallen. And this assistance often comes when we're not even aware of it. "So it may be a part of the great arrangements of divine Providence that many of the most needed and acceptable interpositions for our welfare should come to us from invisible sources, and be conveyed to us from God by unseen hands."[11]

Angels as God's Heavenly Host

Scripture often refers to angels as God's heavenly host.

Micaiah the prophet, for example, said, "I saw the LORD sitting on his throne with all the host of heaven standing on his right and on his left" (2 Chronicles 18:18).

The term *host* has a distinctive military ring to it. And indeed, the Bible often portrays the angels as God's host in military fashion. The word "encompasses the whole array of God's heavenly army and sees them employed as a military force to accomplish His will and do His battles. As such, they are an extension of His power and providence."[12]

The great Reformer John Calvin said that angels are called God's host "because, as bodyguards surround their prince, they adorn his majesty and render it conspicuous; like soldiers they are ever intent upon their leader's standard, and thus are ready and able to carry out his commands. As soon as he beckons, they gird themselves for the work, or rather are already at work."[13]

In addition, the Bible often calls God the "Lord of hosts." David Jeremiah informs us that "more than 250 times in the Bible, God calls himself 'the Lord of hosts,' meaning 'the Lord of Heavenly Armies.'"[14] This title "pictures God as the sovereign commander of a great heavenly army, who works all His pleasure in heaven and earth (cf. 1 Samuel 17:45; Psalm 89:6,8 [KJV])."[15] "This name instantly gives us a royal and military picture of the Lord leading his celestial soldiers."[16] Christians can have a supreme sense of security knowing that this heavenly army, headed by God Himself, is committed to rendering service to them.

Angels as God's Holy Ones

We noted in an earlier chapter that angels are sometimes called *holy ones* (Deuteronomy 33:2; Job 5:1; 15:15; Psalm 89:7; Daniel 4:13,17,23; 8:13; Zechariah 14:5; 1 Thessalonians 3:13; Jude 14). The word *holy* literally means "set apart." The title *holy ones* is appropriate because God's angels are set apart from sin and set apart to God's service.

This is in obvious contrast to the fallen angels (demons) who are *un*holy in every way. They are set apart from righteousness and set apart to the devil to do his unholy bidding. They are against everything related to God.

The angels, as God's holy ones, brought the Law to God's chosen people (Acts 7:53; Galatians 3:19; Hebrews 2:2). God gave the Law to His people so they themselves would pursue holiness—that is, so they would be set apart from the pagan nations around them and be set apart to God. Thus, God used His holy ones (angels) as a means of helping His people become holy too.[17]

Angels as Watchers

Daniel 4:13 (NASB) refers to "watchers." Apparently these are angels who have been sent by God specifically to observe what is transpiring on the earth. The term suggests that these angels are especially vigilant in their activity of watching the affairs of earth.[18] The word *watcher,* in biblical Hebrew, communicates the idea of being "vigilant, making sleepless watch," "to be wakeful," and "on the watch."[19] We might consider the watchers to be God's reconnaissance agents. In his book *All the Angels in the Bible,* Herbert Lockyer says of the watchers, "Having no need of sleep, they are untiringly active in administering their appointed affairs under God's directions."[20]

Some Bible expositors have related the watchers of Daniel 4:13 to other Scripture references that mention the many eyes of certain angels.[21] The cherubim, for example, are "full of eyes" (Ezekiel 1:18). The angels in Revelation 4:6 are likewise "covered with eyes, in front and in back." Verse 8 tells us these angels were "covered with eyes all around, even under [their] wings."

What's in a Title?

We noted at the beginning of this chapter that in ancient times, a name or title was a statement that revealed something about the person bearing it. We have seen that titles tell us a great deal about the nature and function of angels in God's universe.

- Angels are called *sons of God* because they were directly created by God.
- Angels are called *ministering spirits* because they serve human beings in various ways. They help provide protection, guidance, encouragement, and deliverance.
- Angels are called God's *heavenly host* because they function as God's heavenly army employed as a military force to accomplish His will and engage in His battles.
- Angels are called *holy ones* because they are set apart from sin and set apart to service to God.
- Some angels are called *watchers* because of their unique role in observing what is transpiring on planet earth.

We learn a lot about angels by their scriptural titles. But we have yet to look at one extremely important title that comes up quite often in the Old Testament—*the Angel of the Lord*. In the next chapter, our goal will be to identify this "Angel." I think you'll come to agree with me that the Angel of the Lord is one of the most fascinating topics in the entire Bible.

For even though he [Christ] was not yet clothed with flesh [in Old Testament times], he came down, so to speak, as an intermediary, in order to approach believers more intimately. Therefore this closer intercourse gave him the name of angel.

~ John Calvin ~

9

The Angel of the Lord

One of the most fascinating doctrines in the Old Testament has to do with the identity of the Angel of the Lord. This Angel interacts with such Old Testament luminaries as Abraham, Moses, and David. He plays a very significant role in Old Testament history. But who was He?

Having examined all the verses in the Bible that speak about the Angel of the Lord, I am thoroughly convinced that appearances of this Angel in Old Testament times were actually preincarnate appearances of Jesus Christ, the second person of the Godhead. (*Preincarnate* means "before becoming a human being.") As we examine Scripture together, I think you too will come to see that this was no ordinary angel but was in fact the preincarnate Christ.

Theologians call the appearances of Christ in the Old Testament *theophanies.* This word comes from two Greek words: *theos* ("God") and *phaino* ("to appear"). We might define a theophany as an appearance or manifestation of God, usually in visible, bodily form. The principal theophany of the Old Testament is the Angel of the Lord (or, more literally, the Angel of Yahweh). I believe the Angel of the Lord was the primary manifestation of Christ among people who lived prior to His incarnation.

When the Old Testament uses the word *angel* to refer to Christ, the word indicates not a created being (like other angels) but—true to its Hebrew root—a messenger, one who is sent, or an envoy. We will see that Christ, as the Angel of the Lord, was sent by the Father as a messenger or envoy to accomplish specific tasks in Old Testament times. (I'll talk more about the meaning of *angel* later in the chapter.)

How do we know that the Angel of the Lord (or Angel of Yahweh) was actually the preincarnate Christ? We will answer this question with three lines of evidence: (1) This Angel is identified as being Yahweh (or God); (2) though the Angel is identified as being Yahweh, He is also distinct from another person called Yahweh—thus implying plurality within the Godhead; and (3) the Angel of Yahweh must be Jesus Christ by virtue of what we learn from both the Old and New Testaments about the nature and function of each person in the Trinity.

The Angel of Yahweh Is God

In the Old Testament, the Angel of the Lord makes very definite claims to deity. The account of Moses and the burning bush includes a well-known account of this: "Moses was tending the flock of Jethro his father-in-law, the priest of Midian, and he led the flock to the far side of the desert and came to Horeb, the mountain of God. There the angel of the LORD appeared to him in flames of fire from within a bush" (Exodus 3:1-2).

Notice how the Angel identified Himself to Moses: "I am the God of your father, the God of Abraham, the God of Isaac and the God of Jacob" (Exodus 3:6). Upon hearing the Angel's identity, "Moses hid his face, because he was afraid to look at God."

Moses no doubt had in mind the Old Testament teaching that no man can see God and live (Genesis 32:30; Exodus 33:20).

The divine Angel then commissioned Moses to lead the enslaved Israelites out of Egypt. Moses, in the course of his conversation with the Angel, clearly expressed a recognition of divinity: "Moses said to God [the Angel of the Lord], 'Suppose I go to the Israelites and say to them, "The God of your fathers has sent me to you," and they ask me, "What is his name?" Then what shall I tell them?'" (Exodus 3:13).

The Angel then answered with a name that can be used only of God: "God [the Angel of the Lord] said to Moses, 'I AM WHO I AM. This is what you are to say to the Israelites: "I AM has sent me to you"'" (Exodus 3:14). We can hardly conceive of the Angel asserting His deity in any stronger way!

The Angel's deity is also confirmed in Genesis 22. In this chapter we find God instructing Abraham, "Take your son, your only son, Isaac, whom you love, and go to the region of Moriah. Sacrifice him there as a burnt offering on one of the mountains I will tell you about." Just as Abraham was about to slay Isaac, the divine Angel appeared to him and said, "Do not lay a hand on the boy...Do not do anything to him. Now I know that you fear God, because you have not withheld from me your son, your only son." Notice that withholding Isaac from the Angel of the Lord is identical to withholding him from God.

Beyond actual claims to deity, we also find evidences in the Old Testament that the Angel had the attributes of deity. For example, recall what the Angel said to Moses from the burning bush: "Take off your sandals, for the place where you are standing is holy ground" (Exodus 3:5). Of course, the ground itself was not holy. Rather, the holiness was radiating from the divine Angel. His intrinsic holiness required that Moses not defile the surrounding area with his shoes.[1]

The Angel of the Lord also displayed the attributes of omniscience (He was all-knowing) and omnipotence (He was all-powerful). He made promises by His own authority that only God could make.[2] For example, after Hagar fled into the desert to escape from Sarah (Abraham's wife), the divine Angel appeared and promised her, "I will so increase your descendants that they will be too numerous to count" (Genesis 16:10).

No ordinary angel could ever make such a promise. After all, the promise itself required the exercise of omniscience, and fulfilling the promise would require omnipotence.[3] Hagar sensed she was in the presence of God, for she was surprised that she was permitted to live after seeing God (Genesis 16:13).

The Angel of the Lord gave other clear evidences of His divine nature. For example, He had the authority to forgive sins (Exodus 23:21), something only God can do. The Angel also received worship (Joshua 5:14; compare with Exodus 3:5) and accepted sacrifices from people (Judges 13:19-23). He always spoke and acted in His own intrinsic authority (Genesis 16:10). This is in contrast to created angels, who exist to do the bidding of Christ (Colossians 1:16-17).

We could look at many other evidences that prove beyond any doubt the Angel's identity as God. However, these are sufficient to demonstrate that appearances of the Angel of the Lord (Angel of Yahweh) in the Old Testament were, in fact, appearances of God. (My book *Christ Before the Manger: The Life and Times of the Preincarnate Christ* explores this exciting doctrine in great detail.)[4]

Despite our certainty on this, however, we have yet to consider any indication about whether the Angel was an appearance of the triune God, or perhaps one person of the Godhead—the Father, the Son, or the Holy Spirit. We will now begin to narrow the field.

The Angel of Yahweh Is Distinct from Yahweh

We saw earlier that the Angel of the Lord was recognized as being Yahweh (God). However, the divine Angel is also recognized in Scripture as being distinct from another person called Yahweh.

How do we resolve this apparent contradiction? By recognizing trinitarian distinctions in the Godhead! Though the doctrine of the Trinity is not fully revealed until the New Testament, we nevertheless see preliminary glimpses of this important doctrine in the pages of the Old Testament.

For example, in Zechariah 1:12 we find the Angel of Yahweh interceding to another person called Yahweh on behalf of the people of Jerusalem and Judah: "The angel of the LORD [Yahweh] said, 'LORD [Yahweh] Almighty, how long will you withhold mercy from Jerusalem and from the towns of Judah, which you have been angry with these seventy years?' "

What we have here is one person of the Trinity (the second person—the preincarnate Christ as the Angel of the Lord) interceding before another person of the Trinity (the first person—God the Father). As a result of this intercession, the Father reaffirmed His intentions to bless and prosper the chosen people.

We again see trinitarian distinctions in Zechariah 3:1-2. This passage portrays the Angel of Yahweh calling upon Yahweh. Zechariah witnesses the Angel of Yahweh defending Joshua (the high priest) against the accusations of Satan in the presence of Yahweh. In other words, Zechariah sees an Angel called Yahweh speaking to a separate person also called Yahweh! How can two different persons have the name Yahweh? The answer is found in the trinitarian God. One person in the Trinity (the divine Angel, Jesus Christ) was addressing another person in the Trinity (the Father).[5]

Some people might be tempted to argue that because the Angel of Yahweh intercedes to or calls upon Yahweh, He must be less than deity. However, as I point out in *Christ Before the Manger,* the Angel's intercessory prayer to Yahweh and His calling upon Yahweh is no more a disproof of His essential unity with Yahweh than the intercessory prayer of Christ to the Father in John 17 is a disproof of His divinity.[6]

Christ often intercedes to the Father in the New Testament: "He [Jesus] is able to save completely those who come to God [the Father] through him, because he always lives to intercede for them" (Hebrews 7:25). In Jesus, "we have one who speaks to the Father in our defense—Jesus Christ, the Righteous One" (1 John 2:1).

So far, then, we have seen that the Angel of Yahweh *is* Yahweh. We have also seen that the Angel of Yahweh is distinct from another person called Yahweh. These are important foundational truths (trinitarian distinctions) to keep in mind as we continue to narrow our focus regarding the precise identity of the divine Angel.

The Angel of the Lord Is the Preincarnate Christ

How can one person who is clearly identified as God (the Angel of Yahweh) address another person who is just as clearly God (Yahweh)? Since there is only one God, the answer must lie in the personal distinctions of the Trinity. More specifically, the answer lies in recognizing the Angel of the Lord as the second person of the Trinity, Jesus Christ.

A number of fundamental considerations combine to present a strong case for the idea that the Angel of the Lord was actually the preincarnate Christ. Let's take a brief look at five of these considerations.

1. Christ is the visible God of the New Testament, but neither

the Father nor the Holy Spirit characteristically appears visibly. It is true that the Father's voice is heard from heaven, and the Holy Spirit is seen descending as a dove at Jesus' baptism (Matthew 3:16-17). But only Jesus took on visible, bodily form: "The Word became flesh and made his dwelling among us" (John 1:14; compare with Colossians 2:9). We can reasonably assume a consistency between the Old and New Testaments, with Christ being the visible manifestation of God in both Testaments.

Specific statements in the New Testament would seem to support this view. Paul tells us that God the Father is invisible (Colossians 1:15; 1 Timothy 1:17) and "lives in unapproachable light, whom no one has seen or can see" (1 Timothy 6:16). John's Gospel likewise tells us that "no one has ever seen God [the Father], but God the One and Only [Jesus Christ], who is at the Father's side, has made him known" (John 1:18). John 5:37 similarly tells us that no one has ever seen God the Father's form. These passages indicate that the Son's unique function was to make the Father, who has never been seen, known to man.

Scripture also portrays the Holy Spirit as being invisible to the human eye. In the Upper Room Discourse, for example, Jesus said this of the Holy Spirit: "The world cannot accept him, because it neither sees him nor knows him. But you know him, for he lives with you and will be in you" (John 14:17). Believers know the invisible Holy Spirit because He indwells them.

Jesus also said,"The wind blows wherever it pleases. You hear its sound, but you cannot tell where it comes from or where it is going. So it is with everyone born of the Spirit" (John 3:8). The presence of the Holy Spirit is known not by a visible manifestation but by His effect on people.[7]

These facts about the Father and the Holy Spirit point to Christ as being the One who visibly appeared in Old Testament times as the Angel of the Lord.[8] This would seem to be the only interpretation that does full justice to the Scripture passages we've seen.

2. Just as Christ was sent by the Father in the New Testament, so also was the Angel of Yahweh sent by Yahweh in the Old Testament. The divine pattern in Scripture is that the Father is the Sender and the Son is the Sent One.

Of course, this implies no superiority of the Father or inferiority of the Son. This is simply the eternal relationship of the first and second persons of the Trinity. That the Angel and Jesus were both sent by the Father—one in the Old Testament (Judges 13:8-9), the other in the New (John 3:17)—lends support to the idea that they are one and the same person.[9]

3. As we've seen, both the Angel of Yahweh in the Old Testament and Christ in the New Testament interceded to and called upon God the Father. The New Testament pattern is that the second person of the Trinity, Jesus, consistently intercedes to the first person, the Father (see John 17; Hebrews 7:25; 1 John 2:1). This pattern is never reversed in Scripture (that is, we never see the Father interceding to Jesus). The intercessory ministry of the Angel, then, points us to His identity as the preincarnate Christ.[10]

4. The divine Angel and Christ engaged in amazingly similar ministries. Besides interceding for the people of God (Zechariah 1:12-13; 3:1-2; John 17; Romans 8:34; Hebrews 7:25), both the Angel and Christ were involved in revealing truth (Daniel 4:13,17,23; 8:16; 9:21; John 1:1,14,18), commissioning individuals for service (Exodus 3:7-8; Judges 6:11-23; 13:1-21; Matthew 4:18-20; 28:19-20; Acts 26:14-18), delivering enslaved people (Exodus 3; Galatians 1:4; 1 Thessalonians 1:10; 2 Timothy 4:18; Hebrews 2:14-15), comforting the downcast (Genesis 16:7-13; 1 Kings 19:4-8; Matthew 14:14; 15:32-39), protecting God's servants (Psalm 34:7; Daniel 3:15-25; 6:16-22; Matthew 8:24-26), and acting as Judge (1 Chronicles 21:1,14-15; John 5:22; Acts 10:42),

among many other things. These parallel ministries point to the common identity of the Angel and Jesus Christ.

5. The Angel of the Lord no longer appears after the incarnation. This is highly significant. After reading about the active role of the Angel throughout Old Testament history, His sudden disappearance after the incarnation would be strange indeed unless He was a preincarnate manifestation of Jesus Christ. Nothing else explains the Angel's complete inactivity among humans in New Testament times unless He is recognized as continuing His activity as God incarnate—that is, as Jesus Christ.[11]

Some sharp readers may be thinking, *What about the references (albeit few) in the New Testament to "an angel of the Lord"?* Theologian Norman Geisler provides this pivotal insight:

> *An* angel of the Lord (Gabriel) appeared to Joseph (Matthew 1:20); *an* angel of the Lord spoke to Philip (Acts 8:26); and *an* angel of the Lord released Peter (Acts 12:7), but not *the* Angel of the Lord. Furthermore, the New Testament "angel of the Lord," unlike "*the* Angel of the Lord" in the Old Testament, did not permit worship of himself (cf. Revelation 22:8-9), but "*the* Angel of the Lord" in the Old Testament demanded worship (cf. Exodus 3:5; Joshua 5:15).[12]

Distinguishing between *an* angel of the Lord in the New Testament (a created angel) and *the* Angel of the Lord in the Old Testament (the preincarnate Christ) is important. We must be cautious not to get confused between the two.

The View of the Early Church

The early church fathers also believed that appearances of the Angel of the Lord in the Old Testament were actually appearances of the preincarnate Christ. Irenaeus (AD 125–200), a disciple of Polycarp, said in his *Against Heresies* that Christ was often seen by Moses and that it was Christ who spoke to Moses from the burning bush.[13] Irenaeus also said Christ was "implanted everywhere" throughout Moses' writings—interacting with such individuals as Adam, Noah, Abraham, and Jacob.[14]

Church father Justin Martyr (AD 110–166) taught that Christ was extremely active in Old Testament times, dealing with individuals such as Noah, Abraham, Isaac, and Jacob. In one of his writings, Martyr said, "Our Christ conversed with Moses under the appearance of fire from a bush." It was not God the Father who spoke to Moses, but "Jesus the Christ," who "is also God," "the God of Abraham, Isaac, and Jacob," and "the I AM THAT I AM."[15]

Church father and defender of the faith Tertullian (AD 160–220) similarly stated this in *Against Praxeas:*

> It is the Son, therefore, who has been from the beginning administering judgment, throwing down the haughty tower, and dividing the tongues, punishing the whole world by the violence of waters, raining upon Sodom and Gomorrah fire and brimstone, as the LORD from the LORD. For He is who was at all times came down to hold converse with men, from Adam on to the patriarchs and the prophets, in vision, in dream, in mirror, in dark saying.[16]

Other ancient writers who believed the Angel of the Lord was actually the preincarnate Christ include Clement of Alexandria (AD 150–220), Origen (AD 185–254), Theophilus of Antioch (died AD 181), Cyprian (AD 200–258), Hilary (AD 315–367), and Saint Basil (AD 330–379).[17]

A Clue in the Words of Jesus

Did Jesus speak about His preincarnate appearances to anyone during His ministry on earth? He may very well have done just that to the two disciples on the road to Emmaus following His resurrection from the dead: "Beginning with Moses and all the Prophets, he [Christ] explained to them what was said in all the [Old Testament] Scriptures concerning Himself" (Luke 24:27). It seems unlikely that Jesus spoke to the two disciples only about prophecies regarding His coming. We can reasonably assume that He also spoke of His preincarnate appearances.[18]

On another occasion, Jesus told a group of Jews, "If you believed Moses, you would believe me, for he wrote about me. But since you do not believe what he wrote, how are you going to believe what I say?" (John 5:46-47). What Moses wrote (Genesis, Exodus, Leviticus, Numbers, and Deuteronomy) includes not only some prophecies about Christ's future incarnation and ministry (for example, Genesis 3:15; Deuteronomy 18:18) but also some of Christ's preincarnate appearances to humans (for example, Genesis 16:7; 22:11; Exodus 3).

Thus, some passages in the New Testament point to the real possibility that Jesus indeed spoke about His preincarnate appearances to select individuals.

The Meaning of *Angel*

If appearances of the Angel of the Lord in Old Testament times were actually preincarnate appearances of Christ, we should anchor in our minds the precise sense in which He can properly be called an Angel. I alluded to this earlier, but it bears repeating to avoid any confusion.

In accordance with its Hebrew root, the word *angel* was used of Christ in the sense of "messenger," "one who is sent," or "envoy."[19] This usage indicates that Christ was acting on behalf of the Father. Christ, as the Angel of the Lord, was a divine intermediary between God the Father and man.

John Calvin put it this way: "For even though he [Christ] was not yet clothed with flesh, he came down, so to speak, *as an intermediary,* in order to approach believers more intimately. Therefore this closer intercourse gave him the name of angel. Meanwhile, what was his he retained, that as God he might be of ineffable glory."[20] Calvin's point is well taken, for even though Christ may have appeared in the form of an angel, He would forever retain His intrinsic deity and glory.

PART 3

What Angels Do

Even heaven itself has never seen anything so marvelous as the incarnation and the suffering and death of the Creator; nothing so inconceivable as the complete redemption of rebels made to become the church of God.

~ Rene Pache ~

10

Celestial Spectators of Planet Earth

In an earlier chapter we touched on a special class of angels known as *watchers,* whose apparent role is to observe the affairs of earth (Daniel 4:13). Yet Scripture indicates there is a sense in which all angels may be considered celestial spectators of planet earth. The apostle Paul speaks of how the apostles were on display "as a spectacle to the whole universe, to angels as well as to men" (1 Corinthians 4:9). Later he gave instructions to his beloved assistant Timothy "in the sight of God and Christ Jesus and the elect angels" (1 Timothy 5:21).[1] Further, 1 Peter 1:12 tells us that all the angels "long to look into" things related to God's redemption of humankind.

This is a topic of great fascination for the entire angelic realm.[2] We must remember that angels have been observing earth from the very beginning. They were present when man was first created. They witnessed the temptation and fall of Adam and Eve in the Garden of Eden. Throughout the Old

Testament era they witnessed one prophet after another speak about the Redeemer, who would be born in Bethlehem. They witnessed the incarnation and watched as Christ—the One they had served since their creation—took on human flesh. They also witnessed His cruel execution on the cross of Calvary and His glorious resurrection from the dead.

In short, the angels—from the very start—have been celestial spectators of the unfolding drama of human redemption being played out on the earth. Let's take a closer look at what they saw—and what they will see in the days to come.

Witnessing the Creation and Fall of Man

The angels were present when Adam and Eve were created. They heard their beloved God speak the words, "Let us make man in our image, in our likeness, and let them rule over the fish of the sea and the birds of the air, over the livestock, over all the earth, and over all the creatures that move along the ground" (Genesis 1:26). And they beheld God as He constructed man from the dust of the ground and breathed the breath of life into him (Genesis 2:4-7).[3] How awesome this experience must have been for them!

But their awe soon turned to agony when they witnessed the fall of Adam and Eve in the Garden of Eden. As A.C. Gaebelein has so well put it, "With what horror they must have watched when the serpent, Satan, whom they knew so well, sneaked up to the woman and the fatal conversation began. If angels can weep and demons laugh, when sin was born conceived by the liar and murderer from the beginning, angels must have wept in deepest agony, while the demon-world shouted for joy."[4]

Immediately after the Fall, God pronounced judgment against the man, the woman, and Satan (the serpent). But as dark and depressing as this situation was, God also introduced a glimmer of hope into the scenario when He spoke to the serpent of the coming Redeemer: "I will put enmity between you and the woman, and between your offspring and hers; he will crush your head, and you will strike his heel" (Genesis 3:15). The "offspring" of the woman, of course, is a reference to Jesus' future birth as a human being. His work on the cross would deal a fatal blow to Satan and his dark kingdom.[5]

Since that time, the angels have eagerly sought to look into the unfolding drama of human redemption as it is being worked out before their very eyes. From the time they heard the first promise of the Redeemer in Genesis 3:15, they waited with great anticipation for further words of revelation regarding the Promised One. And as God gave revelation, they learned and understood. They saw His unfathomable love toward the lost world of humanity.

Witnessing the Incarnation

The long-awaited day finally arrived. The anticipated moment had come at last. The angels in heaven surrounded the throne and stood in holy awe as the time came for Jesus—their beloved Creator—to veil His glory and take on the creature's form, to be made a little lower than the angels (Philippians 2:6-11; Hebrews 2:9). They stood in deepest reverence as they beheld Jesus about to leave heaven to come to earth to fulfill all that the prophets of God had spoken.

For the previous 400 years, God had given no new revelation to the chosen people, the Jews. Nor had any angels appeared to humans during this time, so far as we know. But now—with the approaching human birth of the Redeemer—angelic activity would increase dramatically.

We will look at this angelic activity in greater detail in chapter 12, "Ministers to Jesus Christ." For now it is sufficient to note simply that the angel Gabriel informed Zechariah that his wife would give birth to John the Baptist, who would prepare the way for the coming Redeemer (Luke 1:13-17). Just a few months later, this same Gabriel was sent from God's throne to announce to Mary that she would give birth to that promised Redeemer (Luke 1:26-35). No greater news was ever sent from the courts of heaven to the lowly realm of earth. The Redeemer, whom the prophets had spoken of for thousands of years, was now about to take on human flesh.

Can you imagine the reverential awe among the angels when they finally beheld the Christ-babe born from the womb of Mary? The memorable night had come. The long-expected child was now cradled in a manger in Bethlehem. The seed of the woman had arrived at last. "All heaven was astir that night. The whole universe filled with the angels of God knows what has taken place. The earth alone is in ignorance of the great event."[6]

But this ignorance would not last long. Following the birth of the Redeemer, a glorious angel appeared to some shepherds living out in the fields nearby. He announced to them that the Redeemer had been born (Luke 2:8-11). Not unexpectedly, the news spread like wildfire.

Witnessing Christ's Earthly Ministry

During Christ's earthly ministry, many people from all different walks of life believed in Him. What a continual source of joy this was for the angels! Indeed, we are told that the angels in heaven rejoice each time a person places faith in Christ and receives the gift of eternal life (Luke 15:7). As Herbert Lockyer puts it, "However lightly the conversion of a soul may be thought of among men, angels receive it with unbounded delight! Nothing so pleases them as the deliverance of a sinner from the power of darkness and his translation into the kingdom of God's dear Son."[7]

The angels must also have uttered shouts of joy every time Jesus—with His omnipotent power—cast a demon (a fallen angel) out of an enslaved human being. They no doubt smiled every time Jesus brought physical healing to a suffering person. And what holy awe they must have felt when they witnessed Him raising people from the dead!

But the angels witnessed other things that must have been difficult to bear. I think of the many people—particularly the religious leaders—who utterly rejected Christ as the Redeemer. How did the angels feel when they saw this? Did they shudder and tremble when they saw cruel and hateful denials of the One they loved and served?

Witnessing the Crucifixion

Perhaps most difficult of all, the angels saw Jesus when He was mocked and cruelly scourged, His face marred and dishonored. Legions of angels likely hovered about Him, wincing in pain as all this occurred. Jesus knew He could have called on these angels to rescue Him (Matthew 26:53), but the Scriptures had to be fulfilled: He had to die on the cross. All heaven must have been affected by what was transpiring on this tiny planet. Creation's Lord was being put to death for the creature's sin!

Finally the work was done. The work of redemption was completed. And just before His death, Jesus triumphantly cried, "It is finished" (John 19:30). These words must have echoed throughout the entire angelic realm: "It is finished…It is finished…It is finished!" Bible expositor Leon Morris tells us, "This is not the moan of the defeated, nor the sigh of patient resignation. It is the triumphant recognition that He has now fully accomplished the work that He came to do."[8] It was indeed finished!

Witnessing the Resurrection and Ascension

Imagine the deafening cheers and applause that must have broken out spontaneously among the angels at the moment of the resurrection. Christ's body had been dead for three days. Then, at a moment in time, He was alive again—forevermore (Luke 24:1-6).

And as Christ ascended into heaven, thousands of angels may have accompanied Him en route. Some scholars see a hint of this in Psalm 68:17-18, which refers to the Lord ascending on high, accompanied by "tens of thousands and thousands of thousands" of angels.

What an awesome moment it must have been when Christ, clothed in a glorified human body, returned to heaven, His natural habitat. What shouts of glory must have then been heard among the cherubim, seraphim, dominions, thrones, powers, and angelic authorities of heaven! A mighty hallelujah chorus no doubt swept through the heavens as He seated Himself "in the heavenly realms, far above all rule and authority, power and dominion, and every title that can be given, not only in the present age but also in the one to come" (Ephesians 1:20-21).[9]

Witnessing the End Times

All the universe is presently in a state of waiting. The spirits of the redeemed in heaven are waiting for that soon-coming day when they will receive their resurrection bodies—bodies that will be immortal and imperishable (1 Corinthians 15:50-53). On the earth, Christ's church—His bride—awaits the coming of the divine Groom. Believers on every continent long for His blessed appearing: "Amen. Come, Lord Jesus" (Revelation 22:20).

When Christ finally comes again, all heaven will be astir. Imagine the commotion that will take place among the angels in heaven as they gather to return to earth with their beloved Creator. And when Christ and the angels arrive on earth, there will be a splendid display of glory (Matthew 25:31). "In that day the earth will become the scene of glory as never before in its history. Angels will then be manifested and be seen in their heavenly glory, the invisible things will become visible."[10] What a day that will be!

God's angels act only to carry out God's commands.
There is no instance of their acting independently.

~ Millard Erickson ~

11

Servants of the Most High

During the angel craze of the 1990s, *Time* magazine exclaimed, "For those who choke too easily on God and his rules... angels are the handy compromise, all fluff and meringue, kind, nonjudgmental. And they are available to everyone, like aspirin."[1] Joan Wester Anderson, author of *Where Angels Walk,* said that "angels are a gateway to spirituality for people who find the Judeo-Christian image of God too threatening."[2] Phyllis Tickle, former religion editor of *Publishers Weekly,* said that "like ecology, angels allow us a safe place to talk to each other about spiritual things. They provide a socially acceptable way to talk about God without stating a theological commitment."[3]

As I write, popular angel books continue to minimize God and exalt angels. We read that with God and the angels, nothing is impossible.[4] We are told that we can pray to our guardian angels to invoke their increased involvement in our lives.[5] If we have a problem with worrying, we can turn solely to the angels for relief. We can also make declarations to the angels regarding what we desire in life, and they will bring it about. (No need to involve God.) Angels can make sure our prayers arrive to God. As well, the angels can bring happiness and fulfillment to our lives. And if we have a heavy load, the angels can lighten it. In fact, we can put our lives on "cruise control" with the angels.[6]

For many people today, the angels take center stage, not God. God is too threatening, too judgmental, many seem to believe. And God demands a commitment. People do not like commitment and talk of a future judgment. Angels, some folks claim, do not carry all this baggage, and this explains why these people have built their entire spiritual lives around angels.

When we turn to the pages of Scripture, however, we find that God is always on center stage and that the angels exist solely to do His sovereign bidding. In fact, as we will soon discover, they never act independently of God.

In the book of Colossians, the apostle Paul gives explicit warnings against angel cults. Apparently, a heresy or cult in Colossae involved the worship of angels. To correct this error, Paul states in Colossians 1:16-17 that Christ is the One who created all things, including all the angels, and therefore, He is supreme and is alone worthy to be worshipped.

Later, in Colossians 2:18, Paul sternly warns against the worship of angels.[7] Elsewhere he warned against worshipping the created in place of the Creator (Romans 1:25). Such passages counter today's overemphasis on angels, for much of what is going on now certainly constitutes a form of angel worship.

We must keep in mind what the psalmist said: "Who in the skies above can compare with the LORD? Who is like the LORD among the heavenly beings?" (Psalm 89:6). In fact, no one is like the Lord, and only He is worthy to be worshipped. An infinite distance separates God and His angels. To ignore this distance is to fall into great theological folly.

We will now briefly examine some key Scriptures regarding angels and their proper relationship to God. In so doing, we will see that much of what some of today's bestselling angel books teach about angels flatly contradicts the Word of God.

Does God Need Angels?

God does not need angels! Don't misunderstand—I don't mean to minimize the importance of what the Bible teaches about angels. I am very thankful that God created angels. My point is simply that God is fully capable of accomplishing His ends without their assistance.

Addressing why God has chosen to use angels to carry out some of His directives in the world, Reformer John Calvin says, "Surely he does not do this out of necessity as if he could not do without them, for as often as he pleases, he disregards them and carries out his work through his will alone."[8] Theologian Charles Ryrie likewise says, "Of course, God is not obliged to use angels; He can do all these things directly. But seemingly He chooses to employ the intermediate ministry of angels on many occasions."[9] Contemporary Bible expositor Tony Evans explains the biblical view with a corporation metaphor: "Angels are God's staff to carry out His will. God manages His universe not as a lone entrepreneur, but as the head of a corporation. God could do it all Himself, but He has chosen to work through His creatures, including both angels and humans."[10]

Though God does not need angels, He nevertheless created them—for His own pleasure and for His own glory—to carry out various functions in His universe and before His throne. What do these functions involve? Among other things, Scripture indicates that God created angels to minister and evidence God's special concern for us as His children (Hebrews 1:14). His use of angels does not detract from His personal love and concern for us but rather is an illustration and expression of it.[11]

Bible scholar Bernard Ramm once made the statement, "We can imagine God as existing without angels, but it is meaningless to imagine a universe with angels but no God."[12] I think Ramm is right (see John 1:3; Hebrews 1:2,10).

In our day, many people act as if angels exist without a personal God to whom we are accountable. Or, if they acknowledge God's existence, they push Him off center stage and relegate Him to a place of irrelevance. These people don't seem to realize that the holy angels themselves insist on humans recognizing that God alone is to remain on center stage (see Revelation 22:8-9).

Unreserved Service to God

At the start of this chapter I quoted an important statement from theologian Millard Erickson: "God's angels act only to carry out God's commands. There is no instance of their acting independently."[13] Erickson is 100 percent correct. Not a single Bible verse portrays an elect, holy angel of God acting independently from Him.

In Scripture, angels are most often described in relation to God as *His* angels (for example, Psalm 104:4). And two angelic names mentioned in the Bible—Michael and Gabriel—emphasize this relationship with God with the *el* ending—which, in Hebrew, means "God."[14] (*Michael* means "Who is like God?" and *Gabriel* means "Mighty one of God.") Angels are *God's* angels, and they exist to carry out His purposes. Psalm 103:20 refers to God's angels as those "who do his bidding, who obey his word."

Throughout Scripture—from the first book in the Bible to the last—we see God sending out angels to accomplish His will. Genesis 19:12-16, for instance, tells us that God sent some angels to destroy the wicked city of Sodom as a judgment. The book of Revelation portrays a number of different angels involved in the outworking of God's sovereign plan in the end times (for example, see chapters 8–10).

We must ever keep in mind, then, that angels are always sent to do God's bidding, and the sent one is never more significant than the divine Sender.[15] In the Bible, God is always in total control, not the angels.

Because the angels are always sent by God on our behalf, our gratitude must go to the God who sent them. God's holy angels do not seek praise or worship for the things they do. In fact, they refuse it and point to God as the only one worthy of worship. When the apostle John wrongly bowed down before an angel in an act of worship, the angel said, "Do not do it! I am a fellow servant with you and with your brothers the prophets and of all who keep the words of this book. Worship God!" (Revelation 22:9).

John Calvin said that "as God does not make [the angels] ministers of his power and goodness to share his glory with them, so he does not promise us his help through their ministry in order that we should divide our trust between them and him." Calvin further stated that the angels "do lead us away unless they lead us by the hand straight to him, that we may look upon him, call upon him, and proclaim him as our sole helper; unless we regard them as his hands that are moved to no work without his direction; unless they keep us in the one Mediator, Christ, that we may wholly depend upon him, lean upon him, be brought to him, and rest in him."[16]

How contrary Calvin's sentiments are to some of today's bestselling books about angels. Indeed, the angels they speak of do not lead us to the God of the Bible.

This brings to mind what the apostle Paul said in 2 Corinthians 11:14-15: "Satan himself masquerades as an angel of light," and the demons who follow him do that as well. I am convinced that many of the angels who are so popular among some of today's angel enthusiasts are nothing less than demonic spirits—fallen angels.

Of course, this is not to downplay or minimize the importance of genuine appearances and activities of the holy angels. I believe such appearances do occur and that angels are active in our world today. But when today's ideas about angels are tested against Scripture (1 Thessalonians 5:21), many of them do not measure up. Reader beware!

Glorious Praise and Worship to God

Scripture reveals that a primary function of angels is to worship and praise Almighty God. In fact, some angels unceasingly praise God day and night. Revelation 4:8, for example, tells us, "Each of the four living creatures [angels] had six wings and was covered with eyes all around, even under his wings. Day and night they never stop saying: 'Holy, holy, holy is the Lord God Almighty, who was, and is, and is to come'" (compare with Isaiah 6:3).

Scripture gives the distinct impression that the angels give this praise audibly, as they did at the birth of Jesus Christ (Luke 2:13-14).[17] Imagine, then, the glorious sound that greeted the apostle John's ears when he witnessed 100 million angels singing praises in unison to the God they adore:

> I looked and heard the voice of many angels, numbering thousands upon thousands, and ten thousand times ten thousand. They encircled the throne and the living creatures and the elders. In a loud voice they sang: "Worthy is the Lamb, who was slain, to receive

> power and wealth and wisdom and strength and honor and glory and praise!" (Revelation 5:11-12).

Someday, we who are believers will receive glorified bodies and join the countless multitude of angels in singing praise to God. That's a day to look forward to!

If the angels exert such a ministry in regard to Christ, it is because they are particularly subordinated to Him. Like all other creatures, they were made by Him and for Him.

~ Rene Pache ~

12

Ministers to Jesus Christ

Paul states in Colossians 1:16 that everything in the universe—including every angel—was created by Christ and for Christ. All things were created for Christ's glory, for such purposes as He sovereignly designed. He built the universe to be His own property, to be the theater in which He could accomplish His purposes and display His infinite perfections.[1]

As we examine what Scripture says about angels, we see more and more clearly just what Colossians 1:16 means when it says the angels were created for Christ. Indeed, we find numerous occasions in the Bible where the angels are heartily engaged in various duties for Christ or on His behalf. Scholar Edward Myers notes that "of one hundred seventy-five references in the New Testament to angels, fifty-one are found in the synoptic Gospels [Matthew, Mark, and Luke]. Many of these references are to the work or mission of angels in the life of Christ."[2]

In this chapter we will take a close look at these duties, which include the worship and praise of Christ, the announcements of Christ's birth to Mary and to Joseph, the proclamation of Christ's birth to the shepherds, angelic intervention during the earthly life of Jesus, and angelic involvement at the crucifixion, resurrection, ascension, and second coming of Christ.

Worshipping the Preincarnate Christ

Some 700 years before Christ was born in Bethlehem, we find a fascinating account of the angels worshipping Him in His preincarnate state. We read about this glorious event in chapter 6 of the book of Isaiah. While Isaiah was in the temple, he had a vision in which he found himself in the presence of God's glory:

> In the year that King Uzziah died, I saw the Lord seated on a throne, high and exalted, and the train of his robe filled the temple. Above him were seraphs [angels], each with six wings: With two wings they covered their faces, with two they covered their feet, and with two they were flying. And they were calling to one another: "Holy, holy, holy is the LORD Almighty; the whole earth is full of his glory."
>
> At the sound of their voices the doorposts and thresholds shook and the temple was filled with smoke. "Woe to me!" I cried. "I am ruined! For I am a man of unclean lips, and I live among a people of unclean lips, and my eyes have seen the King, the LORD Almighty" (Isaiah 6:1-5).

This passage is rich in meaning. We find the prophet Isaiah in the temple in 740 BC, perhaps mourning the death of godly King Uzziah. Isaiah may have gone there to pray in his grief.

While Isaiah was in the temple, God granted him a glorious vision that would give him strength for the duration of his ministry. The prophet saw the Lord seated on a throne, "high and exalted" (Isaiah 6:1) and adorned in a long and flowing robe that pointed to His kingly majesty. Though an earthly king had died, the true King of the universe still reigned supreme from on high.

Isaiah saw seraphs above God's throne (Isaiah 6:2-3). These were magnificent angels who proclaimed God's holiness and glory. As we noted earlier in the book, the term *seraph* comes from a root word meaning "to burn," emphasizing the burning passion of these angelic beings to serve their King.

These angels covered their faces with their wings in God's presence. Despite their own brightness and purity, they apparently could not look at the greater brightness and purity of God, who—as the New Testament tells us—dwells in "unapproachable light" (1 Timothy 6:16).

The seraphs proclaimed, "Holy, holy, holy is the LORD Almighty" (Isaiah 6:3). Triple repetition is often used in Scripture to emphasize a truth, and in this case, it points to the fullness or completeness of God's holiness.

At the sound of the angels' voices, the doorposts and the thresholds shook, and the temple was filled with smoke (Isaiah 6:4). Human encounters with God often involved the presence of smoke (see Exodus 20:18-19). This smoke was no doubt the cloud of glory, which Isaiah's ancestors had seen in the wilderness (Exodus 13:21; 16:10) and which the priests in Solomon's day had viewed in the temple at its dedication (1 Kings 8:10-13).

All this becomes extremely significant when we read in John's Gospel that what Isaiah actually saw was Jesus' glory (John 12:41). The words of Isaiah 6:3 refer to the glory of "the LORD Almighty" (or, more literally, the Yahweh of hosts), but John says these words actually refer to Jesus Christ. Jesus and Yahweh are here equated.

How awesome this must have been for Isaiah! About 700

years before the Messiah was born in Bethlehem, Isaiah saw the glory of the preincarnate Christ in a vision. And the One whom Isaiah had personally encountered in this vision is the same One whose human birth he prophesied (Isaiah 4:2; 7:14; 9:6-7; 11:1-5,10; 32:1; 42:1-4; 49:1-7; 52:13–53:12; 61:1-3). The One Isaiah beheld in this vision—worshipped by the holy angels—is the same One those same angels would serve when He became a human being in Bethlehem.

Announcing the Birth to Mary

For several hundred years, God's voice through the prophets had been silent in Palestine. The Roman army had nearly crushed the Jews' hopes that the promised Messiah would come to deliver them. Had God forgotten His people? Many people might have thought so. But when the proper time came, something glorious happened. An angel from heaven appeared to Mary with some incredible news.

The first chapter of Luke's Gospel tells us about this annunciation (announcement):

> In the sixth month, God sent the angel Gabriel to Nazareth, a town in Galilee, to a virgin pledged to be married to a man named Joseph, a descendant of David. The virgin's name was Mary. The angel went to her and said, "Greetings, you who are highly favored! The Lord is with you" (verses 26-28).

Earlier in man's history, the angel Gabriel had given Daniel special revelations from God regarding the coming Messiah (Daniel 8:16; 9:21). Now, more than 500 years later, this same angel appeared to Mary with the news that the promised Messiah would be born by her, a virgin. This was in fulfillment of

Isaiah 7:14, which prophesied that the Messiah would be born of a virgin.

Following Gabriel's announcement, Mary was "greatly troubled at his words and wondered what kind of greeting this might be" (Luke 1:29). Apparently, in her modesty and humility, Mary did not understand why a glorious heavenly angel would come to greet her in such exalted terms and tell her that the Lord was with her.

Gabriel then said, "Do not be afraid, Mary, you have found favor with God. You will be with child and give birth to a son, and you are to give him the name Jesus. He will be great and will be called the Son of the Most High. The Lord God will give him the throne of his father David, and he will reign over the house of Jacob forever; his kingdom will never end" (Luke 1:30-33).

Although Gabriel calmed Mary's initial fears, his message probably created additional concerns for her. Would Joseph believe the impossible? What would their friends and neighbors think when they learned that Mary was pregnant? Would she be branded as the worst of sinners rather than God's chosen instrument? Perhaps those questions filled her mind as the heavenly angel spoke to her. Through it all, however, Mary maintained an attitude of faith and obedience.

Gabriel's pronouncement that the child would be called *Jesus* is full of meaning. The name *Jesus* means "the Lord saves" or "the Lord is salvation." The name points to the very reason that Christ became a human being—to save His people.

Besides informing Mary of the Savior's name, Gabriel also told her that Jesus would be great, He would be called the Son of the Most High, and He would reign on the throne of His father David. Each of these three descriptions reveals something important about Jesus' true identity. For example, the term *great* is a title that, when unqualified, is usually reserved for God alone.[3]

Being called "the Son of the Most High" is significant, for *Most High* is a title often used of God in both the Old and New Testaments (for example, Genesis 14:19; 2 Samuel 22:14; Psalm 7:10; Acts 7:48). Bible expositor John A. Martin comments on this:

> Mary could not have missed the significance of that terminology. The fact that her Baby was to be called the "Son of the Most High" pointed to His equality with God. In Semitic thought a son was a "carbon copy" of his father, and the phrase "son of" was often used to refer to one who possessed his "father's" qualities.[4]

This Great One—eternal God in human flesh—would rule, according to Gabriel, on the throne of David. Jesus, who in His humanity was a direct descendant of David (Matthew 1:1), will rule from David's throne during the future 1000-year millennial kingdom in perfect righteousness and peace (2 Samuel 7:16; Psalm 89:3-4,28-37). This kingdom will begin immediately after the second coming of Christ (Revelation 19).

Gabriel used three words in Luke 1:32-33 to describe this future rule of Christ: *throne, house,* and *kingdom* ("The Lord God will give him the throne of his father David, and he will reign over the house of Jacob forever; his kingdom will never end"). Each of these words is included in the covenant that God made with David—a covenant in which God promised that someone from David's line would rule forever (2 Samuel 7:16).

Gabriel's words must have brought these Old Testament promises to mind for Mary, who was a devout young Jew. Indeed, Gabriel's message constituted "an announcement as clear as it was possible to make it that Mary's son would come into this world to fulfill the promise given to David that one of David's sons would sit on David's throne and rule over David's kingdom."[5] Jesus would come not only to be the Savior but also to be the Sovereign.

Mary then responded to Gabriel by inquiring, "How will this be…since I am a virgin?" (Luke 1:34). The angel answered, "The Holy Spirit will come upon you, and the power of the Most High will overshadow you. So the holy one to be born will be called the Son of God. Even Elizabeth your relative is going to have a child in her old age, and she who was said to be barren is in her sixth month. For nothing is impossible with God" (verses 35-37). Though Mary had not asked Gabriel for a sign, he revealed that God's power was already at work by mentioning Mary's relative Elizabeth, who had long been barren but was now pregnant with John the Baptist in her womb.

How overwhelming the announcement of the incarnation must have been for young Mary! We cannot know the kinds of emotions she must have felt at the moment of Gabriel's revelation that eternal God would be in her womb. But Mary responded in a humble manner: "I am the Lord's servant," she said. "May it be to me as you have said" (Luke 1:38).

In her heart, Mary may have quietly prayed, *My life's priorities have suddenly been changed. My wedding plans must be laid aside. I am willing to face shame and ridicule. Whatever You say, Lord, I accept.*

Announcing the Birth to Joseph

When Joseph discovered that Mary was pregnant, he had two options, neither of which was marriage. (As a righteous man, he could not think of marrying a woman who was carrying what he presumed to be another man's child.) One option was to publicly accuse Mary of immorality and have her stoned to death

(Deuteronomy 22:13-21). Her death would break the betrothal contract. A second alternative open to Joseph was to divorce Mary (breaking a betrothal required a divorce). Because Joseph was a righteous man and did not want to expose Mary to public disgrace, he decided to divorce her quietly (Matthew 1:19).

But then an angel appeared to Joseph in a dream and informed him that the baby in Mary's womb was of the Holy Spirit (Matthew 1:20).[6] This was no earthly conception or pregnancy, he was told. What God had planned in eternity past, He was now fulfilling in Joseph's wife-to-be. The angel said, "She will give birth to a son, and you are to give him the name Jesus, because he will save his people from their sins" (Matthew 1:21). In the original Greek text, the last part of this verse is especially emphatic: "It is He and no other who will save His people from their sins."

The angel's revelation to Joseph was necessary because Mary was in a humanly impossible situation. She knew she had been faithful to Joseph, yet she had also submitted to God's will to make her the human mother of the divine-human Messiah. She never could have adequately explained to Joseph what had happened, so God sent an angel to Joseph to explain what was going on. The angel's announcement defended Mary's moral integrity so Joseph could marry her in good conscience.

When Joseph awoke from the dream, he did as the angel had commanded him and took Mary home as his wife. Joseph willingly violated Jewish custom by immediately taking her into his home rather than waiting until the one-year betrothal period had passed. However, as the Bible tells us, "he had no union with her until she gave birth to a son. And he gave him the name Jesus" (Matthew 1:25). That Joseph "had no union" with Mary until Jesus was born emphasizes that Jesus had no human biological father.[7]

Like Mary, Joseph must have been overwhelmed by the revelation he had received from the angel. The Messiah would be born from his wife's womb! "The eternal Son of the eternal God had existed as One with the Father from all eternity. The One who by his power had created the universe would come in human flesh through Mary's womb. Jesus Christ, the eternal One, reached out through his birth and took to himself a true and complete humanity. He united true humanity and true deity in one person forever. Such was the revelation given to Joseph."[8]

Proclaiming the Arrival to the Shepherds

In dire contrast to Jesus' intrinsic glory and majesty, He was born in lowly conditions and placed in a manger. But His majesty was acknowledged in other ways. Following His birth, a glorious angel appeared to some shepherds living out in the fields nearby to make an announcement of monumental importance—the Messiah had been born.

We can hardly imagine the scene as the darkness of the night was suddenly dissipated by the glorious appearance of this angel. Understandably, the shepherds were terrified at what they beheld (Luke 2:9).

The angel immediately comforted them and told them not to be afraid. After all, he had come not as a minister of death but as a proclaimer of life to "all the people" (Luke 2:10). This recalls Genesis 12:3, which declares the prophetic announcement that "all peoples on earth" would be blessed through the coming of the Messiah.

The angel then made an astonishing statement: "Today in the town of David [Bethlehem] a Savior has been born to you; he is Christ the Lord" (Luke 2:11). Keep in mind that according to the Old Testament, God is the only Savior of His people.

God said, "I, even I, am the LORD, and apart from me there is no Savior" (Isaiah 43:11). As we have seen, Christ the babe is called "Savior" in Luke 2:11. This is a powerful testimony to Christ's identity as God.

Note that the angel told the shepherds that "Christ *the* Lord" had been born, not "Christ *your* Lord." Christ is the Sovereign not just of men but of angels as well.[9] Christ is the Lord, in an unqualified sense, over all creation (Colossians 1:16).

As the angel continued speaking to the shepherds, suddenly and without warning "a great company of the heavenly host appeared with the angel, praising God and saying, 'Glory to God in the highest, and on earth peace to men on whom his favor rests' " (Luke 2:13-14). These angels had known and served Christ in His preincarnate state. And now, following the virgin birth, they praised God because the One they had known and served for so long had just been born as a human being—a tiny babe in Bethlehem.

After the angels departed into heaven, the shepherds said to one another, "Let's go to Bethlehem and see this thing that has happened" (Luke 2:15). English cannot easily convey the sense of urgency that is present in the original Greek text of this verse. We might paraphrase it, "Come on, let us make haste and quickly go and see."[10] The shepherds were excited about the angel's message, no doubt partly because of the widespread messianic expectations in first-century Judaism. They knew a Messiah was coming, but now they had received word that He was here!

After the shepherds saw the divine Babe, "they spread the word concerning what had been told them about this child, and all who heard it were amazed at what the shepherds said to them" (Luke 2:17-18). The Greek word translated *amaze* means "to wonder," "to be astonished." The word conveys the idea that when people heard the testimony of the shepherds, they had goose bumps on their skin and tingles down their spines. The prophesied Messiah had now come—eternal God in human flesh!

Ministering to Christ on Earth

The Gospel accounts indicate that the holy angels actively ministered to Jesus in various ways throughout His earthly life.

Christ's infancy. The first instance of angelic intervention happened when evil King Herod tried to put an end to baby Jesus' life. Herod did not want any competitors to his throne. His goal, therefore, was to remove any possibility of a future king of the Jews. He wanted to put Jesus to death.

To foil Herod's attempt to kill Jesus, an angel appeared to Joseph and instructed the family to flee to Egypt. Joseph at once obeyed the command and went to Egypt, where he and his family remained until Herod died (Matthew 2:13-18).

Following Herod's death, an angel appeared to Joseph in a dream and said, "Get up, take the child and his mother and go to the land of Israel, for those who were trying to take the child's life are dead" (Matthew 2:20). So Joseph took his family back to the land of Israel, where Jesus was raised.

What can we learn from this account? First, God—in His omniscience—knows the hearts, desires, and plans of all men, including evil rulers like Herod. And second, the angels carried out the sovereign bidding of God by communicating messages and warnings to Joseph and his family. God the Father undertook the providential care of His Son during His infancy through the ministry of angels.

Christ's early ministry. Jesus' public ministry was inaugurated at His baptism in the River Jordan (Matthew 3). Following His baptism, the Spirit led Him into the desert to be tempted by the devil (Matthew 4:1). Satan's purpose in tempting Jesus was to thwart God's plan of redemption by disqualifying the Savior. But God's purpose was to prove that Jesus was a sinless and worthy Savior.

Scripture tells us that following the temptations, "the devil left him, and angels came and attended him" (Matthew 4:11). The word *attended* comes from a Greek word meaning "to serve," "to wait upon," "to care for someone's needs."[11] This is what the angels did for Jesus. Following this 40-day period of intense temptations, the angels served Him, waited upon Him, and cared for His needs.

At Gethsemane. Just prior to His arrest the night before His crucifixion, Jesus was in the Garden of Gethsemane feeling the tremendous weight of what was ahead of Him. After He prayed to the Father, an angel appeared from heaven and strengthened Him (Luke 22:43). The word *strengthened* in this verse literally means "to invigorate," "to cause to be strong," "to make firm."[12] This angel performed a vital ministry for Christ just prior to His going to the cross to die for the sins of humankind.

At the crucifixion. During the arrest in the garden, one of the disciples drew a sword to defend Jesus. But Jesus responded by saying, "Do you think I cannot call on my Father, and he will at once put at my disposal more than twelve legions of angels?" (Matthew 26:53). A Roman legion had 6000 soldiers; twelve legions of angels would thus amount to 72,000 angels.

Jesus' point, of course, was that if He so desired, He could have called upon innumerable angels to deliver Him. But He chose not to do this so He could go to the cross and secure salvation for humankind. Evangelist Billy Graham offered this comment:

> The angels would have come to the cross to rescue the King of kings, but because of His love for the human

race and because He knew it was only through His death that they could be saved, He refused to call for their help. The angels were under orders not to intervene at this terrible, holy moment. Even the angels could not minister to the Son of God at Calvary. He died alone in order to take the full death penalty you and I deserved.[13]

Serving at the Resurrection

After Jesus died on the cross, His body was buried in accordance with Jewish burial customs. He was wrapped in a linen cloth with about 100 pounds of aromatic spices that were mixed together to form a gummy substance.

After His body was placed in a solid-rock tomb, an extremely large stone was rolled against the entrance with the help of levers. This stone would have weighed up to four tons (8000 pounds). It wouldn't have been easily moved by human beings.

Roman soldiers guarded the tomb. These strictly disciplined men were highly motivated to follow their orders successfully. Fear of cruel punishment produced flawless attention to duty, especially in the night watches. These Roman guards would have affixed the Roman seal on the tomb, a stamp representing Rome's sovereign power and authority.

All this security at the tomb makes the situation following Christ's resurrection highly significant. The Roman seal had been broken, an offense that carried an automatic penalty of crucifixion upside down for the person who did it. Moreover, the large stone was now a substantial distance from the entrance, as if it had been plucked out of the way like a pebble. The Roman guards had fled. The penalty for a Roman guard leaving his position was death, so we can assume they must have had a good reason for fleeing!

We learn the details of what happened in Matthew 28:1-6:

> After the Sabbath, at dawn on the first day of the week, Mary Magdalene and the other Mary went to look at the tomb. There was a violent earthquake, for an angel of the Lord came down from heaven and, going to the tomb, rolled back the stone and sat on it. His appearance was like lightning, and his clothes were white as snow. The guards were so afraid of him that they shook and became like dead men.
>
> The angel said to the women, "Do not be afraid, for I know that you are looking for Jesus, who was crucified. He is not here; he has risen, just as he said."

The rest is history. The women, filled with joy, ran to tell the disciples the glorious news: Christ has risen!

Appearing at the Ascension

Christ later ascended into heaven as some of His disciples watched (Acts 1:9). Just as He was ascending, two angels appeared to the disciples and said, "Men of Galilee...why do you stand here looking into the sky? This same Jesus, who has been taken from you into heaven, will come back in the same way you have seen him go into heaven" (verse 11). The angels—as messengers of God—indicated to the disciples that just as Jesus had visibly and physically ascended into heaven, so also would He visibly and physically come again at the second coming.

Descending at the Second Coming

Scripture consistently tells us that when Christ visibly and physically returns to earth, a vast host of angels will accompany Him. Matthew 16:27 says that "the Son of Man is going to come in his Father's glory with his angels." Matthew 25:31 tells us, "When the Son of Man comes in his glory, and all the angels with him, he will sit on his throne in heavenly glory." Second Thessalonians 1:7 speaks of Christ coming again "in blazing fire with his powerful angels." What a resplendently glorious scene this will be!

Exalting Christ for All Eternity

Earlier we saw that angels continuously worship Christ. One of the most glorious Scripture passages dealing with this is Revelation 5:11-14. We close this chapter with these words from the apostle John:

> I looked and heard the voice of many angels, numbering thousands upon thousands, and ten thousand times ten thousand. They encircled the throne and the living creatures and the elders. In a loud voice they sang: "Worthy is the Lamb, who was slain, to receive power and wealth and wisdom and strength and honor and glory and praise!"
>
> Then I heard every creature in heaven and on earth and under the earth and on the sea, and all that is in them, singing: "To him who sits on the throne and to the Lamb be praise and honor and glory and power, forever and ever!" The four living creatures said, "Amen," and the elders fell down and worshiped.

Believers, look up—take courage.
The angels are nearer than you think.

~ Billy Graham ~

13

Angels Among *Us*

The angels are nearer than you think. They're all around us, taking care of us and ministering to us when we're not even aware of their presence. What comfort we as believers can gain from this inspiring biblical teaching!

Simply because we are not living in biblical times does not mean the angels have ceased their activities among us. As one Bible scholar put it, "There is not a shred of biblical evidence that points to their sudden withdrawal from human affairs. God has not 'recalled' the angels...Neither are they dormant. The Bible still says that angels are sent to be ministering spirits to *those who will inherit salvation* (Heb. 1:14). If that isn't you and me, then who is it?"[1]

A vast world of intelligent, powerful, invisible spirit beings is all around us and warrants careful study. By understanding what Scripture says about the doctrine of angels, believers become aware of one of the most exciting ways God takes care of us during our earthly sojourns.

As we have seen, we must base our understanding of this

subject on Scripture alone. John Calvin once said that the error in much angelology is that it deals with angels apart from the biblical witness.[2] This is precisely what has happened on a popular level today. Many of the current bestselling angel books contain legend, lore, and outright occultism in regard to angels, but they pay little attention to what God's Word teaches on the subject.

In this chapter, we will discover what Scripture says about some of the important ways God uses angels to minister to believers. In the process, may your faith in God and His mighty provisions for your life be strengthened.

The Ministry of Angels to Believers

Hebrews 1:14, as we have noted earlier, says that angels are "ministering spirits sent to serve those who will inherit salvation." But in what ways do angels minister to the heirs of salvation?

Among many other things, God may use angels to answer a believer's prayer (Acts 12:7). Sometimes they give encouragement in times of danger (Acts 27:23-24), and they take care of believers at the moment of death (Luke 16:22; Jude 9). The ministry of angels to believers is wide and varied.

John Wesley, the eighteenth-century founder of Methodism, wrote that angels serve humankind "in a thousand ways...They may assist us in our searching after truth, remove many doubts and difficulties...They may warn us of evil in disguise, and place what is good in a clear strong light."[3]

Because angels are so active in the believer's life, evangelist Billy Graham says, "Every true believer in Christ should be encouraged and strengthened! Angels are watching; they mark your path. They superintend all the events of your life and protect the interest of the Lord God, always working to promote His plans and to bring about His highest will for you." Indeed, Graham says, if we "would only realize how close His ministering angels are, what calm assurance we could have in facing the cataclysms of life. While we do not place our faith directly in angels, we should place it in the God who rules the angels; then we can have peace." Let us be clear on this: Many millions of angels are at God's command to render service to the heirs of salvation. "The hosts of heaven stand at attention as we make our way from earth to glory, and Satan's BB guns are no match for God's heavy artillery."[4]

God's Invisible Helpers

Most people generally walk by sight and not by faith—that is, they live their lives and interpret reality according to what is tangibly real to their physical senses. Of course, if we limit our understanding of reality to the physical world, we remain ignorant of the vast world of invisible spirit beings around us.

We see a number of examples in the Bible that illustrate how people often don't perceive angels. Recall that when an angel stopped Balaam, at first only the donkey saw him standing with a drawn sword in his hand (Numbers 22:23,31). The Lord had to open Balaam's eyes before he could see the angel.

The prophet Elisha and his servant provide another example in 2 Kings 6:15-17:

> When the servant of the man of God got up and went out early the next morning, an army with horses and chariots had surrounded the city. "Oh, my lord, what shall we do?" the servant asked. "Don't be afraid," the prophet answered. "Those who are with us are more than those who are with them." And Elisha prayed, "O LORD, open his eyes so he may see." Then

> the LORD opened the servant's eyes, and he looked and saw the hills full of horses and chariots of fire all around Elisha.

Elisha alone perceived the presence of the heavenly host that had come to help him. He had to pray and ask God to reveal the angels to his frightened servant (whom I've often envisioned to look like Don Knotts). Like the servant, you and I may often be unaware of the presence of angels. We'll never know how many times God has kept us safe through the work of angels without us having known anything about it. "Even though you can't see or hear your guardian angel, he can see and hear you."[5]

As Billy Graham so aptly put it, "Often [angels] may be our companions without our being aware of their presence. We know little of their constant ministry. The Bible assures us, however, that one day our eyes will be unscaled to see and know the full extent of the attention angels have given us (1 Corinthians 13:11-12)."[6]

The Sadducees—who seemed to walk more by sight than by faith—are the only group in the Bible who didn't believe in angels (Acts 23:8). Their treatment of the apostles is amusingly ironic. In Acts 5:17-18 we read that "the high priest and all his associates, who were members of the party of the Sadducees, were filled with jealousy. They arrested the apostles and put them in the public jail." But then—you guessed it—an angel delivered them from jail: "During the night an angel of the Lord opened the doors of the jail and brought them out. 'Go, stand in the temple courts,' he said, 'and tell the people the full message of this new life'" (verses 19-20). The apostles must have smiled to ponder God's sense of humor in all this.

God's Messengers

We noted earlier in this book that the word *angel* literally means "messenger." This points to a primary role of the angels. They serve as God's messengers, bringing revelation, announcements, warnings, and other information to the people of God.

Angels appeared to Lot to warn him about the impending judgment on Sodom (Genesis 19). An angel appeared to the prophet Daniel to reveal the future (Daniel 9). An angel appeared to Zechariah to announce the coming birth of John the Baptist (Luke 1:13). Angels appeared to Joseph and Mary to announce the birth of the Savior, Jesus Christ (Matthew 1; Luke 1). An angel appeared to Cornelius and instructed him to send for Simon Peter so Peter could tell him all about salvation in Jesus Christ (Acts 10:3-33). All throughout the pages of Scripture, we find angels appearing to human beings as God's messengers.[7]

We must not forget that when the angels act as messengers, they are always and in every way *God's* messengers. David Jeremiah is right when he says that the angels "are couriers for Someone other than themselves. They're Someone else's ambassadors, Someone else's agents. They represent only Him, and never themselves. They are channels to carry only His information. They speak and act according to His instructions and they bear His authority." Indeed, "they are *His* messengers. When they give us strength or enlightenment, it is God's strength or enlightenment that they impart. Their encouragement is God's encouragement. Their guidance is God's guidance. Their protection is God's protection. When they bring comfort, it is God's comfort they offer. And when they bring wrath, it is God's wrath they inflict."[8]

Guardians of God's People

Without a doubt, the most popular and controversial aspect of the study of angels has to do with their role as the guardians of God's people. Some Bible scholars say every believer has a specific assigned guardian angel who stays with him or her throughout life, while others believe that angels in general are assigned to watch over believers in general.

Two primary passages in the New Testament relate to the idea of guardian angels. Matthew 18:10, speaking of children, says, "See that you do not look down on one of these little ones. For I tell you that their angels in heaven always see the face of my Father in heaven." Then, in Acts 12:15, we find a servant girl named Rhoda recognizing Peter's voice outside the door of the house, and the people inside—thinking Peter was still in jail—saying, "You're out of your mind...It must be his angel." Some theologians have concluded from these two verses that every believer must have his or her own guardian angel.

Many of the early church fathers, for example, believed that every individual is under the care of a particular angel who is assigned to him or her as a guardian. Likewise, the great philosopher and theologian Thomas Aquinas said that each person has a guardian angel assigned to him or her at birth. Prior to the birth of the child, Aquinas said, the child in the womb falls under the care of the mother's guardian angel.[9]

The idea of individual guardian angels for each person is particularly popular today among New Age angel enthusiasts. The line of thinking here is that not only Christians but all people on earth have guardian angels—regardless of whether they believe in the Christ of the Bible.

Why have guardian angels become so popular today? Writer David Connolly offers this answer:

> Human life is often mysterious and frightening, and there is sometimes a profound need in us for a belief in attentive caring and protection greater than what

> can come from ourselves alone—an inner security gently extended from a higher love and wisdom to sustain us through the fears and dangers of human experience.[10]

Perhaps many today want to believe in guardian angels so they can feel secure in an often chaotic and crime-ridden world.

Of course, the Scriptures teach that angels are ministering spirits not to those who reject Christ but only to the "heirs of salvation"—that is, Christians (Hebrews 1:14). This verse alone causes the New Age view of guardian angels to tumble like a house of cards.

Matthew 18:10 and Acts 12:15 may possibly imply that each believer has a specific guardian angel assigned to him or her, but many theologians argue that this is flimsy support for such an idea.[11] (For example, they point out that the angels of the little ones in Matthew 18:10 are said to be *in heaven,* not specifically *with* the little ones.)[12] These theologians argue that Scripture seems to indicate that many multitudes of angels are always ready and willing to render help and protection to each individual Christian whenever a need arises. Perhaps John Calvin put it best:

> Whether individual angels have been assigned to individual believers for their protection, I dare not affirm with confidence...Specific angels have been appointed as guardians over kingdoms and provinces. Christ also, when he says that the children's angels always behold the Father's face [Matthew 18:10], hints that there are certain angels to whom their safety has been committed. But from this I do not know whether one ought to infer that each individual has the protection

> of his own angel. We ought to hold as a fact that the care of each one of us is not the task of one angel only, but all with one consent watch over our salvation.[13]

Calvin believes that we should feel happy and confident knowing that many angels are constantly guarding us, rather than feel discouraged because we don't each have an individual angel:

> If the fact that all the heavenly host are keeping watch for his safety will not satisfy a man, I do not see what benefit he could derive from knowing that *one* angel has been given to him as his special guardian. Indeed, those who confine to one angel the care that God takes of each one of us are doing a great injustice both to themselves and to all the members of the church.[14]

Calvin says God "not only promises to take care of us, but tells us he has innumerable guardians whom he has bidden to look after our safety; that so long as we are hedged about by their defense and keeping, whatever perils may threaten, we have been placed beyond all chance of evil." Indeed, he says, "Angels are dispensers and administrators of God's beneficence toward us...They keep vigil for our safety, take upon themselves our defense, direct our ways, and take care that some harm may not befall us." The angels "are ever ready to bring help to us with incredible swiftness, should circumstance require it, even as lightning sent forth from heaven flies to us with its usual speed."[15]

The idea that many angels watch after us seems to have some support in Scripture. For example, we read in 2 Kings 6:17 that Elisha and his servant were surrounded by many glorious angels. Luke 16:22 indicates that several angels carried

Lazarus's soul to Abraham's bosom. Jesus could have called on 12 legions of angels to rescue Him if He had wanted (Matthew 26:53). Psalm 91:9-11 tells us, "If you make the Most High your dwelling—even the LORD, who is my refuge—then no harm will befall you, no disaster will come near your tent. For he will command his angels concerning you to guard you in all your ways."

Whether each of us has just one angel watching over us or many, we cannot say for sure. Yet one thing is certain: If we as Christians were more fully aware of God's provision of angelic protection (regardless of how many angels are involved), we would most certainly be less fearful of our circumstances and enemies. Our big problem, of course, is that we tend to walk by sight and not by faith. The walk of faith recognizes God's constant provision of angelic protection.[16]

This is indeed *God's* provision. Only because of God do we have such protection. The angels are quick to watch after us only because of their complete and unrestrained loyalty to God. As Lewis Sperry Chafer put it, "The faithful service of angels to mankind cannot be explained on the grounds of their love for humanity. They are interested in that which concerns their God."[17] Charles Spurgeon likewise comments: "Angels are unseen attendants of the saints of God: they bear us up in their hands lest we dash our foot against a stone. Loyalty to their Lord leads them to take a deep interest in the children of His love."[18]

Ministers Who Answer Prayer

Certainly God does not have to depend on angels in order to answer the prayers of His people. In fact, oftentimes He answers prayer apart from any angelic involvement (see, for example, 1 Chronicles 5:20; 1 Peter 3:12). Nevertheless, God sometimes sovereignly chooses to use angels when answering people's prayers.

In Acts 12, we find Peter wrongfully imprisoned. We read that while Peter was in jail, "the church was earnestly praying to God for him" (verse 5). What happened next? All of a sudden, an angel appeared in Peter's prison cell and helped him escape:

> He struck Peter on the side and woke him up. "Quick, get up!" he said, and the chains fell off Peter's wrists. Then the angel said to him, "Put on your clothes and sandals." And Peter did so. "Wrap your cloak around you and follow me," the angel told him. Peter followed him out of the prison, but he had no idea that what the angel was doing was really happening; he thought he was seeing a vision. They passed the first and second guards and came to the iron gate leading to the city. It opened for them by itself, and they went through it. When they had walked the length of one street, suddenly the angel left him (Acts 12:7-10).

Clearly, here is an example of Christians praying to God and God immediately responding by dispatching an angel to grant the request. We must assume that God sometimes answers our prayers in this way as well. When we petition the throne of God with a prayer request, God may sovereignly grant that request, assigning a specific angel to bring it about.

We should be aware that demons (fallen angels) sometimes seek to thwart the angels God uses in the process of answering a particular prayer. We read about one such incident in the book of Daniel.

According to Daniel 10:13, an angel that God had sent to answer Daniel's prayer was detained by a more powerful fallen angel (a demon). Only when the archangel Michael showed up to render aid was the lesser angel freed to carry out his task. One lesson we learn from this account is that we must be fervent in our prayers and not think that God is not listening simply because of an apparent delay in His answer.

Escorts at the Moment of Death

Death has been called the great equalizer. Regardless of whether a person is a man or a woman, rich or poor, thick or thin, black or white, all humans are equal in that they eventually die.

For the Christian, God has taken the sting out of death (1 Corinthians 15:55). Because of what Christ has accomplished for us, death is simply a transition during which our spirits leave our physical bodies and enter directly into the presence of Christ. In a way, then, death is a glorious event.

Perhaps one of the most meaningful ministries angels have to us as believers is that at the very moment of death, they accompany us into heaven (Luke 16:22). When that glorious separation of the spirit from the body takes place, the angels are there to personally escort us into our eternal inheritance.[19] The angels will give us a royal welcome as we enter the presence of God.

Billy Graham describes the glory of what awaits the believer in the next life: "The wonders, beauties, splendor, and grandeur of heaven will be yours. You will be surrounded by these heavenly messengers sent by God to bring you home where you may rest from your labors, though the honor of your works will follow you (Revelation 14:13)."[20]

That will be a glorious day.

An Awesome Presence

Our discussion of the work of angels among believers would

not be complete without at least a passing recognition of the awesomeness of angelic appearances. In Scripture, believers who were visited by angels frequently responded with great fear during the first few moments. This doesn't mean we should fear angels. (Obviously, we're not to fear angels; we're to praise God that He has made these glorious provisions for our well-being.) But we must question many of the bestselling angel enthusiasts today, who teach that angel appearances are always nonthreatening and easy to take.

According to current literature, angel appearances can allegedly take the form of nudgings, intuition, or coincidence. They can appear as light on the water, or in clouds and rainbows. They can even appear as a swan. In fact, we are told that angel appearances can "take whatever form the visited person is willing to accept."[21]

Contrary to this, the Bible gives no indication whatsoever that angels appear to humans according to whatever form people are willing to accept. Rather, the visitation of angels typically involves a glorious and awesome appearance that brings fear and trembling to a person.

For example, when Daniel saw an angel he was left without strength (Daniel 10:8).[22] Zechariah was gripped with fear when an angel appeared to him while he was in the temple (Luke 1:12). The shepherds in the field were very much afraid when an angel appeared to them (Luke 2:9). The Roman soldiers trembled with fear and became as dead men when an angel appeared and rolled back the stone blocking Jesus' tomb (Matthew 28:2-4).

So we see that angelic appearances in biblical times were so awesome and so glorious that people naturally responded with fear. God's holy angels are magnificent and beautiful beings, and man is not accustomed to their overwhelming appearance.

Of course, despite the awesome and glorious appearance of angels, Scripture consistently emphasizes that we are never to worship them. As we noted earlier, the apostle Paul explicitly condemns the worship of angels in Colossians 2:18. The angels themselves refuse worship and affirm that God alone is worthy of such honor (Revelation 19:10; 22:8-9). God Himself explicitly commands that only He is to be worshipped (Exodus 20:5-6).

Rejoicing in God's Provision

In this chapter we have tried to reach a balanced and biblical understanding of the work angels have among believers. We've looked not only at angels' various ministries among us but also at the proper attitude we are to have toward them. Perhaps theologian Charles Hodge sums it up best with these words:

> This Scriptural doctrine of the ministry of angels is full of consolation for the people of God. They may rejoice in the assurance that these holy beings encamp round about them, defending them day and night from unseen enemies and unapprehended dangers. At the same time they must not come between us and God. We are not to look to them nor to invoke their aid. They are in the hands of God and exercise His will.[23]

The work of angels among believers is truly an exciting doctrine, for it points to God's great concern for us. Billy Graham therefore exhorts us, "Believers, look up—take courage. The angels are nearer than you think."[24] Amen!

Then I heard a loud voice from the temple saying to the seven angels, "Go, pour out the seven bowls of God's wrath on the earth."

~ Revelation 16:1 ~

14

Angels Among *Them*

Many angel enthusiasts have claimed that interacting with angels is a way of being spiritual without having to necessarily involve God. Bestselling angel author Sophy Burnham suggests that "we have created this concept of God as punitive, jealous, judgmental." She assures us that "angels never are. They are utterly compassionate."[1]

Terry Lynn Taylor, in her recent book *Messengers of Love, Light, and Grace,* claims that "the main lesson the angels have for us is that we are love, we are God on earth, and it is time to love ourselves and open our hearts."[2] There is no need for negativity of any kind.

Regardless of what form an angelic appearance may take, we are told, the messages from angels are always positive. Indeed, Burnham says the typical message from an angel is, "Don't be afraid, everything is just fine."[3] After all, as another recent book put it, "with God and his angels, nothing…is impossible."[4]

We are also told that one way to tell whether we have encountered an angel has to do with the aftereffects of angelic visitations. Burnham, for example, says that a common mark of an angelic visitation is that it "brings a calm and peaceful serenity that descends sweetly over you, and this is true even when the angel is not seen."[5]

Alma Daniel, Timothy Wyllie, and Andrew Ramer, authors of *Ask Your Angels,* agree, suggesting that "feelings of love, of greater self-acceptance, of inner peace, of being deeply cared for and recognized, are signs of angelic connection."[6] Even if we don't see anything tangible, angelic presence can be detected by these characteristics. Burnham even claims, "On three different occasions I have actually felt them all hug me, not as we know hugging, with arms, but an embrace with their whole being; and I feel tingly and a surge of pure electrical love runs throughout my whole body."[7]

From reading such literature on angels, we might believe that angels have nothing but good news, blessing, and happiness for the entire world of human beings. This, however, is not the picture of angels the Scriptures portray. Certainly we read of the great positive benefit of angelic involvement in the lives of believers, but for those who reject the Christ of the Bible, it is a different story altogether.

Promoting Evangelism

On at least one occasion in the New Testament, an angel guides an evangelist (Philip) to a sinner (an Ethiopian treasurer) (Acts 8:26). In Acts 10:1-8, an angel guides a sinner (Cornelius) to an evangelist (Peter).[8] In both incidents, God used angels to assist in the work of evangelism.[9]

Such angelic involvement in evangelistic activity may not be a normative, everyday occurrence for Christians. But given the need and the circumstances, even today God may choose on occasion to providentially utilize His holy angels to bring sinners and evangelists together.

We learn from this that God loves sinners so much that, when conditions warrant it, He is willing to go to extreme means to reach people with the message of the Gospel. This puts an exclamation point on what we read in 2 Peter 3:9, which says that God does not want anyone to perish.

Restraining Wickedness

On at least a few occasions in Scripture, God's holy angels restrain evil. For example, in the book of Genesis we read about some angels who struck a group of wicked men with blindness so the men couldn't carry out their evil intentions when they came to Lot's house (Genesis 18:22; 19:1,10-11).[10] The angels then helped Lot and his family escape from Sodom prior to the judgment that fell on that wicked city (19:14-15).

Might God's angels have acted in the past to restrain some evil from befalling you? I'd say absolutely! Think back to the true story in chapter 1 regarding the missionary John Paton and his wife, who lived on the New Hebrides Islands. Hostile natives were set to attack the missionary headquarters one night, but the Patons prayed to God, and the natives suddenly turned away and left. Paton later found out that the tribe had refrained from attacking because they saw that the headquarters was surrounded by hundreds of "men," all dressed in shining garments with swords drawn.[11]

When we get to heaven and fellowship face-to-face with God's holy angels, perhaps we will discover that they acted to restrain some evil from befalling us many times in the course of our day-to-day affairs. We should be thankful to God for this angelic ministry.

Announcing Judgments

We noted earlier that some angels helped Lot and his family escape from Sodom before the city was destroyed. This sobering event is a great example of how God uses angels to announce impending judgments. On this occasion the angels said to Lot, "We are going to destroy this place. The outcry to the LORD against its people is so great that he has sent us to destroy it" (Genesis 19:13).

In the book of Revelation we see that God's angels will announce judgments throughout the future seven-year tribulation period (which will follow the rapture of the church). For example, in Revelation 14—prior to the outpouring of God's seven bowl judgments on the earth—we read that an angel will fly through the air proclaiming with a loud voice, "Fear God and give him glory, because the hour of his judgment has come. Worship him who made the heavens, the earth, the sea and the springs of water" (verse 7). Another angel will follow and make this announcement:

> If anyone worships the beast and his image and receives his mark on the forehead or on the hand, he, too, will drink of the wine of God's fury, which has been poured full strength into the cup of his wrath. He will be tormented with burning sulfur in the presence of the holy angels and of the Lamb (verses 8-10).

At the very end of the tribulation period, the angels will make still another announcement of judgment. The apostle John describes this for us:

> I saw an angel standing in the sun, who cried in a loud voice to all the birds flying in midair, "Come, gather together for the great supper of God, so that you may eat the flesh of kings, generals, and mighty men, of horses and their riders, and the flesh of all people, free and slave, small and great" (Revelation 19:17-18).

What can we deduce from all this? For one thing, angel enthusiasts who say that the typical message from an angel is, "Don't be afraid, everything is just fine. There is nothing but love," are in gross error.[12] Though angels are loving and do bring comfort to the people of God, they also bring messages of death, destruction, and judgment to those who reject Christ.

Executing Judgment

Angels not only announce God's impending judgments but also execute them. A prime example of this is in Acts 12. Here we read that one day, Herod put on his royal robes, sat on his throne, and delivered a public address to the people. His listeners then shouted, "This is the voice of a god, not of a man" (Acts 12:22). Verse 23 tells us what happened next: "Immediately, because Herod did not give praise to God, an angel of the Lord struck him down, and he was eaten by worms and died." In this case, God gave an angel authority to take a human being's life in judgment.

During the tribulation, God will use His angels to execute many judgments against an unbelieving world. For example, according to Revelation 8, angels are involved in the seven trumpet judgments that are poured out on humankind. In these judgments, hail and fire will fall on the earth, a third of the earth will burn up, the sea will turn into blood, a third of the living creatures in the sea will die, the waters of the earth will become undrinkable, and much more will happen (see verses 5-13).

Likewise, we read in Revelation 16:1, "I heard a loud voice from the temple saying to the seven angels, 'Go, pour out the seven bowls of God's wrath on the earth.'" These particular judgments, which will be inflicted by angels, will result in such horrors as painful sores, death, unbearably intense heat from the sun, darkness over the land, and a violent earthquake (see verses 2-18). The tribulation will truly be a frightening time to be living on this planet.

Reaping the Harvest

In His parable of the weeds, Jesus speaks about sowing good seed in a field, pulling up weeds and burning them, and bringing in the harvest. In Matthew 13:37-43, He explains the symbolism of this parable:

> The one who sowed the good seed is the Son of Man. The field is the world, and the good seed stands for the sons of the kingdom. The weeds are the sons of the evil one, and the enemy who sows them is the devil. The harvest is the end of the age, and the harvesters are angels. As the weeds are pulled up and burned in the fire, so it will be at the end of the age. The Son of Man will send out his angels, and they will weed out of his kingdom everything that causes sin and all who do evil. They will throw them into the fiery furnace, where there will be weeping and gnashing of teeth.

This sobering passage tells us that at the end of the age, God's angels will actually take hold of Christ-rejecting evildoers and "throw them into the fiery furnace." Tragically, modern angel enthusiasts fail to recognize this somber but extremely important aspect of the work of angels.

No matter how many pleasures Satan offers you,
his ultimate intention is to ruin you.
Your destruction is his highest priority.

~ Erwin Lutzer ~

15

Fallen Angels

The biblical evidence for the existence and activity of Satan and demons is formidable. Seven books in the Old Testament specifically teach the reality of Satan (Genesis, 1 Chronicles, Job, Psalms, Isaiah, Ezekiel, and Zechariah). Every New Testament writer and 19 of the books make specific reference to him (for example, Matthew 4:10; 12:26; Mark 1:13; 3:23,26; 4:15; Luke 11:18; 22:3; John 13:27). Jesus Christ refers to Satan some 25 times.

Some people throughout church history have claimed that Satan is not a real person—an idea no doubt inspired by Satan himself. After all, without a real enemy, no one will prepare for defense. And with no preparation for defense, the enemy can attack at will and work his evil while remaining incognito.

The Bible is just as certain of Satan's existence as of God's existence. It reveals that Satan is both a fallen angel and a genuine person. How do we know he is a person? The Scriptures reveal that Satan has all the attributes of personality—including mind (2 Corinthians 11:3), emotions (Luke 22:31; Revelation 12:17), and will (Isaiah 14:12-14; 2 Timothy 2:26). Not only that, but personal pronouns are used to describe him (Job 1; Matthew 4:1-12). As well, Satan performs personal actions (Matthew 4:1-11; John 8:44; 1 John 3:8; Jude 9).

The Scriptures portray Satan as a created being who is powerful but has definite limitations. Satan does not possess attributes that belong to God alone, such as omnipresence (being everywhere-present), omnipotence (being all-powerful), and omniscience (being all-knowing). Satan is a creature, so he is lesser than (and is responsible to) the Creator. Satan can only be in one place at one time, his strength (though great) is limited, and his knowledge (though great) is limited.

Even though Satan possesses creaturely limitations, Scripture nevertheless pictures him as being extremely powerful and influential in the world. He is the "ruler of this world" (John 12:31 NASB), "the god of this world" (2 Corinthians 4:4 KJV), and the "prince of the power of the air" (Ephesians 2:2 KJV). He deceives the whole world (Revelation 12:9; 20:3). He has power in the governmental realm (Matthew 4:8-9; 2 Corinthians 4:4), the physical realm (Luke 13:11,16; Acts 10:38), the angelic realm (Ephesians 6:11-12; Jude 9), and the ecclesiastical (church) realm (Revelation 2:9; 3:9). Clearly, Christians should be very concerned about Satan.

Where did Satan and the demons come from? Did God create Satan and demons as evil beings, or were they holy at one time? These are critical questions that demand good answers.

Evidence for Lucifer's Fall

The fall of Lucifer, and the angels who followed his lead, changed the course of cosmic history. Bible scholar Herbert Lockyer describes the fall this way:

> The apostasy of angels is clearly taught in different parts of Scripture. A vast number of intelligent beings, how many we have no way of knowing, lost their pristine honor and happiness, their primeval virtue and dignity. Excelling all others in knowledge, power, and splendor, they rose up in rebellion against the Creator, Benefactor, and Sovereign and sunk to the depths of sin, shame, and misery, earning for themselves thereby endless hatred and contempt. Like the devil, their leader, they too were drowned in conceit. Through pride they fell, and since their fall they have labored to effect universal rebellion against the laws of God. Dreadful punishment awaits these angels transformed into evil, malignant spirits and demons.[1]

Many Bible scholars through the centuries have believed that Ezekiel 28 and Isaiah 14 contain a description of Lucifer's fall. Let's briefly consider these passages.

Ezekiel 28:11-19—Pride and Judgment

The first ten verses of Ezekiel 28 appear to deal with a human leader. Then, starting in verse 11 and continuing through verse 19, Lucifer is the focus of discussion.[2] Let's briefly look at these latter verses.

> The word of the LORD came to me: "Son of man, take up a lament concerning the king of Tyre and say to him: 'This is what the Sovereign LORD says:
>
> "'You were the model of perfection, full of wisdom and perfect in beauty.
>
> You were in Eden, the garden of God; every precious stone adorned you: ruby, topaz and emerald,

chrysolite, onyx and jasper, sapphire, turquoise and beryl.

Your settings and mountings were made of gold; on the day you were created they were prepared.

You were anointed as a guardian cherub, for so I ordained you.

You were on the holy mount of God; you walked among the fiery stones.

You were blameless in your ways from the day you were created till wickedness was found in you.

Through your widespread trade you were filled with violence, and you sinned.

So I drove you in disgrace from the mount of God, and I expelled you, O guardian cherub, from among the fiery stones.

Your heart became proud on account of your beauty, and you corrupted your wisdom because of your splendor.

So I threw you to the earth; I made a spectacle of you before kings.

By your many sins and dishonest trade you have desecrated your sanctuaries.

So I made a fire come out from you, and it consumed you, and I reduced you to ashes on the ground in the sight of all who were watching.

All the nations who knew you are appalled at you; you have come to a horrible end and will be no more.'"

What is the rationale for the conclusion that these verses refer to the fall of Lucifer? Notice that after the first ten verses in this chapter, which speak about the ruler of Tyre (who was condemned for claiming to be a god though he was just a man), the discussion then moves to the king of Tyre starting in verse 11. The switch from *ruler* to *king* and the allusions to the Garden of Eden seem to imply that the individual described here was more than human.[3] Many scholars believe that though there was a human ruler of Tyre, the real king of Tyre was Satan, for he was ultimately at work in this wicked, anti-God city, and he worked through the human ruler of the city.

Some scholars have suggested that these verses may actually be dealing with a human king of Tyre who was empowered by Satan. Charles Ryrie, for example, suggests that "the historic king of Tyre was simply a tool of Satan, possibly indwelt by him. And in describing this king, Ezekiel also gives us glimpses of the superhuman creature, Satan, who was using, if not indwelling, him."[4]

Thomas Ice and Robert Dean, in their book *Overrun by Demons,* note that in Scripture Satan is sometimes "addressed through the creature he is influencing. For example, when Jesus foretold His crucifixion, Peter began to rebuke Him. But Jesus rebuked Peter and said, 'Get behind Me, Satan!' (Matthew 16:23). In addition, when God pronounced a curse on Satan in Genesis 3:14-15 He addressed Satan indirectly through the serpent."[5] So even though Ezekiel 28:11-19 refers to a king, the ultimate subject of these verses may be Satan.

Note also that some things about this king cannot ultimately be true of human beings.[6] For example, the king had a different nature than man had (he is a cherub, considered to be in the inner circle of angels with closest access to God, Ezekiel 28:14); he had a different position than man had (he was blameless and sinless, verse 15); he was in a different realm than man was in (he was on the holy mount of God, verses 13-14; see also Genesis

3:1-7); he received a different judgment than man received (he was cast out of the mountain of God and thrown to the earth [verse 16], which seems to parallel the description of Satan's fall in Revelation 12); and the superlatives used to describe him don't seem to fit a human being ("full of wisdom," "perfect in beauty," and having "the model of perfection," verse 12).

Our text tells us that this king was a created being and left the creative hand of God in a perfect state (Ezekiel 28:12,15). "God did not create Satan as some prime minister of evil. As with all God's Creation, Satan was a perfectly created being—one of the crowning achievements in God's angelic realm."[7]

One theologian has suggested that Lucifer "awoke in the first moment of his existence in the full-orbed beauty and power of his exalted position, surrounded by all the magnificence which God gave him. He saw himself as above all the hosts in power, wisdom, and beauty. Only at the throne of God itself did he see more than he himself possessed...Before his fall he may be said to have occupied the role of prime minister for God, ruling possibly over the universe but certainly over this world."[8]

Ezekiel 28 tells us that this king was perfect in his ways until iniquity was found in him (verse 15). What was this iniquity? We read in verse 17, "Your heart became proud on account of your beauty, and you corrupted your wisdom because of your splendor." Lucifer apparently became so impressed with his own beauty, brilliance, intelligence, power, and position that he began to desire for himself the honor and glory that belonged to God alone. The sin that corrupted Lucifer was self-generated pride.

Apparently, this represents the actual beginning of sin in the universe—preceding the fall of the human Adam by an indeterminate time. Sin originated in the free will of Lucifer, who—with full understanding of the issues involved—chose to rebel against the Creator.

God rightfully judged this mighty angelic being: "I threw you to the earth" (Ezekiel 28:17). This doesn't mean that Satan had no further access to heaven, for other Scriptures clearly indicate that Satan maintained this access even after his fall (for example, Job 1:6-12; Zechariah 3:1-2). However, Ezekiel 28:17 indicates that Satan was completely cast out of God's heavenly government and his place of authority (see Luke 10:18).

One final evidence: All that is said of this king of Tyre in Ezekiel 28 is elsewhere stated in Scripture of the person of Lucifer or Satan.

Isaiah 14:12-17—Pretender to the Divine Throne

Isaiah 14:12-17 is another Old Testament passage that many scholars believe refers to the fall of Lucifer:

> How you have fallen from heaven, O morning star, son of the dawn!
>
> You have been cast down to the earth, you who once laid low the nations!
>
> You said in your heart, "I will ascend to heaven; I will raise my throne above the stars of God; I will sit enthroned on the mount of assembly, on the utmost heights of the sacred mountain. I will ascend above the tops of the clouds; I will make myself like the Most High."
>
> But you are brought down to the grave, to the depths of the pit.
>
> Those who see you stare at you, they ponder your fate: "Is this the man who shook the earth and made kingdoms tremble, the man who made the world a desert, who overthrew its cities and would not let his captives go home?"

Some Bible scholars see no reference whatsoever to Lucifer in this passage.[9] They argue that the being mentioned in this verse is referred to as a man (Isaiah 14:16) and is compared with other kings on the earth (verse 18). They believe that the statement, "How you have fallen from heaven" (verse 12) refers to a fall from great political heights.[10]

Other scholars interpret this passage as referring *only* to the fall of Lucifer, with no reference whatsoever to a human king. The argument here is that the description of this being is beyond humanness and therefore could not refer to a mere mortal man.

I think a third view is preferable to the two views above. This view sees Isaiah 14:12-17 as having a dual reference. Verses 4 through 11 may deal with an actual king of Babylon. Then, in verses 12 through 17, we find a dual reference that includes not only the king of Babylon but also a typological description of Lucifer.

If Isaiah 14 does indeed contain a reference to the fall of Lucifer, the pattern of this passage would seem to fit that of the Ezekiel 28 reference—that is, it first describes a human leader and then refers to both a human leader and Satan.

The language used to describe this being fits other passages in the Bible that speak about Satan. For example, the five "I wills" in Isaiah 14 indicate an element of pride, which we also see in Ezekiel 28:17 (see also 1 Timothy 3:6, which makes reference to Satan's conceit). Let's examine this pride in more detail by looking at the five "I wills" in Isaiah 14:13-14 and considering how each may indicate something about Lucifer's fall:

"I will ascend to heaven." Apparently Lucifer wanted to abide in heaven and desired equal recognition alongside God Himself.

"I will raise my throne above the stars of God." The "stars" likely refer to the angels of God. Lucifer apparently desired to rule over the angelic realm with the same authority as God.

"I will sit enthroned on the mount of assembly, on the utmost heights of the sacred mountain." Scripture elsewhere indicates that "mount of assembly" refers to the center of God's kingdom rule (see Isaiah 2:2; Psalm 48:2). The phrase is sometimes associated with the Messiah's future earthly rule in Jerusalem during the millennial kingdom. Satan may have desired to rule over humans in place of the Messiah.[11]

"I will ascend above the tops of the clouds." In the Bible, clouds often metaphorically represent the glory of God (Exodus 13:21; 40:28-34; Matthew 26:64; Revelation 14:14). Apparently Lucifer sought a glory equal to that of God Himself.

"I will make myself like the Most High." Scripture describes God as the possessor of heaven and earth (Genesis 14:18-19). Apparently Lucifer sought the supreme position of the universe for himself. "Satan wanted to be as powerful as God. He wanted to exercise the authority and control in this world that rightfully belongs only to God. His sin was a direct challenge to the power and authority of God."[12]

If Isaiah 14:12-17 is a reference to the fall of Lucifer, as I believe it is, then we should emphasize that Lucifer's sin against God is especially vile and wicked for several reasons. First, this was the first example of sin in the universe. Lucifer was the first to fall. Second, God originally created Lucifer in a state of beauty and perfection. He had everything going for him, but he corrupted himself. Third, Lucifer had incredibly great intelligence and was certainly aware that he would suffer consequences for rebelling against the Creator. And fourth, Lucifer enjoyed perfect fellowship with the Creator.[13] Despite living in such a perfect environment, however, Lucifer still rebelled against the One who brought him into being.

Satan's sin, of course, had widespread effects. "It affected other angels (Revelation 12:7); it affects all people (Ephesians 2:2); it positioned him as the ruler of this world (John 16:11); it affects all the nations of the world, for he works to deceive them (Revelation 20:3)."[14] Satan's act of rebellion had unfathomable consequences.

As a result of this heinous sin against God, Lucifer was banished from living in heaven (Isaiah 14:12). He became corrupt, and his name changed from *Lucifer* ("morning star") to *Satan* ("adversary"). His power became completely perverted (Isaiah 14:12,16-17). Following the second coming of Christ, he will be bound in a pit during the 1000-year millennial kingdom over which Christ will rule (Revelation 20:3). Eventually, he will be thrown into the lake of fire (Matthew 25:41).

A key question that has fascinated Bible students throughout the centuries has to do with *when* Lucifer fell. Scripture does not pinpoint for us when this horrendous event occurred. However, it had to be before the events described in Genesis 3 (the temptation of Adam and Eve) because Satan (formerly Lucifer) took part in that temptation (2 Corinthians 11:3). The most we can say, then, is that Lucifer's fall took place sometime prior to the fall of Adam and Eve.

How Scripture Describes Satan

It is fascinating to study the various ways the Bible speaks about Satan. Indeed, we learn much about him and his work by the various names and titles Scripture uses for him.

Accuser of the brethren (Revelation 12:10). The Greek text of this verse indicates that accusing God's people is a continuous, ongoing work of Satan. He never lets up; he accuses God's people "day and night." Thomas Ice and Robert Dean note that "Satan opposes God's people in two ways. First, he brings charges against believers before God (Zechariah 3:1;

Romans 8:33). Second, he accuses believers to their own conscience."[15]

Adversary (1 Peter 5:8 KJV). This word indicates that Satan opposes us and stands against us in every way he can.

Beelzebub (Matthew 12:24). This word literally means "lord of the flies," carrying the idea "lord of filth." The devil corrupts everything he touches.

Devil (Matthew 4:1). This word carries the idea of "adversary" as well as "slanderer." Satan was and is the adversary of Christ; he is the adversary of all who follow Christ. He slanders God to man (Genesis 3:1-7) and man to God (Job 1:9; 2:4). A slanderer utters malicious and false reports that injure the reputation of another.[16]

Enemy (Matthew 13:39). This term comes from a root word meaning "hatred." It characterizes Satan's attitude in an absolute sense. He hates both God and His children.

Evil one (1 John 5:19). He is "the opposer of all that is good and the promoter of all that is evil."[17] Indeed, he is the very embodiment of evil.

Father of lies (John 8:44). The word *father* is used here metaphorically of the originator of a family or company of persons animated by a deceitful character. Satan was the first and greatest liar.

Murderer (John 8:44). This word literally means "man killer" (see 1 John 3:12,15). Hatred is the motive that leads a person to commit murder. Satan hates both God and His children, so he has a genuine motive for murder. Ray Stedman notes that "because he is a liar and a murderer, the Devil's work is to deceive and to destroy. There you have the explanation for all that has been going on in human history throughout the whole course of the record of man...Whom the Devil cannot deceive, he tries to destroy, and whom he cannot destroy, he attempts to deceive."[18]

God of this age (2 Corinthians 4:4). Of course, this does not mean that Satan is deity. It simply means this is an evil age, and Satan is its god in the sense that he is the head of it. Also, as god of this age, Satan is in "back of the false cults and systems that have cursed the true church through the ages."[19]

Prince of the power of the air (Ephesians 2:2 KJV). The "air" in this context appears to be the world we live in. This realm represents the very seat of Satan's authority.

Prince of this world (John 12:31; 14:30; 16:11). The key term here is *world*. This word refers not to the physical earth but to "a vast order or system that Satan has promoted which conforms to his ideals, aims, and methods."[20]

Roaring lion (1 Peter 5:8-9). This graphic simile depicts Satan's strength and destructiveness.

Tempter (Matthew 4:3). "This name indicates his constant purpose and endeavor to incite man to sin. He presents the most plausible excuses and suggests the most striking advantages for sinning."[21]

Serpent (Genesis 3:1; Revelation 12:9). This word symbolizes the origin of sin in the Garden of Eden as well as the hatefulness and deadly effect of sin. The serpent is characterized by treachery, deceitfulness, venom, and murder.

This brief survey of names and titles makes it clear that Satan's avowed purpose is to thwart the plan of God in every area he can and by every means possible. Toward this end, Satan promotes a world system that he rules and that stands in full opposition to God.

Satan's Vast Experience

Christians need to realize that Satan has vast experience bringing people down. In fact, Charles Ryrie explains that his experience is far greater than any person's has ever been.

> By his very longevity Satan has acquired a breadth and depth of experience which he matches against the limited knowledge of man. He has observed other believers in every conceivable situation, thus enabling him to predict with accuracy how we will respond to circumstances. Although Satan is not omniscient, his wide experience and observation of man throughout his entire history on earth give him knowledge which is far superior to anything any man could have.[22]

Because of his vast experience, Satan knows what will likely work in his attempt to foul you up. He is a master tempter who, for thousands of years, has successfully lured humans into sin. Christian beware!

Satan as "the Ape of God"

Augustine first called the devil *Simius Dei*—"the ape of God." Satan is the great counterfeiter.[23] He mimics God in many ways. "The principal tactic Satan uses to attack God and His program in general is to offer a counterfeit kingdom and program."[24] Paul hints at this in 2 Corinthians 11:14, where he says Satan masquerades as an angel of light.

In what ways does Satan act as "the ape of God"?

- Satan has his own church—the "synagogue of Satan" (Revelation 2:9).
- Satan has his own ministers—ministers of darkness who bring false sermons (2 Corinthians 11:4-5).
- Satan has formulated his own system of theology—called "doctrines of demons" (1 Timothy 4:1 NASB; see also Revelation 2:24).
- His ministers proclaim his gospel—"a gospel other

than the one we preached to you" (Galatians 1:7-8).

- Satan has his own throne (Revelation 13:2) and his own worshippers (13:4).
- Satan inspires false christs and self-constituted messiahs (Matthew 24:4-5).
- Satan employs false teachers who bring in "destructive heresies" (2 Peter 2:1).
- Satan sends out false prophets (Matthew 24:11).
- Satan sponsors false apostles who imitate the true (2 Corinthians 11:13).

In view of such mimicking, one theologian has concluded that "Satan's plan and purposes have been, are, and always will be to seek to establish a rival rule to God's kingdom. He is promoting a system of which he is the head and which stands in opposition to God and His rule in the universe."[25]

Satan's Attempts to Thwart Christ

As we trace the history of the New Testament, we see Satan's dark agenda to thwart the person and mission of Jesus Christ. Consider the following historical facts:

According to Matthew 2, Joseph, Mary, and Jesus had to flee to Egypt—having been warned by an angel—because Herod ordered the slaughter of all male children, hoping to kill Christ in the process (verses 13-16). The account in Matthew does not mention the involvement of Satan, but it was nevertheless a satanic act. Revelation 12:4-6 supports the idea that Satan sought Jesus' death shortly after His birth.

Following His baptism, Jesus was led into the wilderness,

where He was tempted by the devil for 40 days (Matthew 4:1-11). Of course, Christ is God and could not be made to sin. But Satan still attempted to disqualify Christ from being the Savior.

During some of His encounters with Israel's religious leaders, Jesus saw the work of Satan in their actions. For example, some of the Jewish leaders sought to have Jesus put to death. Jesus responded, "You belong to your father, the devil, and you want to carry out your father's desire. He was a murderer from the beginning" (John 8:44).

Jesus also saw the work of Satan among those He was closest to. For example, when Jesus predicted His own death, Peter rebuked Him and said, "Never, Lord!...This shall never happen to you!" (Matthew 16:22). Jesus then said to Peter, "Get behind Me, Satan!" (verse 23 NASB). Jesus saw Peter's words as Satan's attempt to stop Him from going to the cross.

These and other verses indicate that the devil did everything he could to thwart the mission of Jesus Christ. The spiritual warfare must have been brutal; we can't possibly know just how much spiritual warfare our Lord must have encountered on the road to Calvary.

The Six Judgments of Satan

Within the pages of Scripture we find six distinct judgments against Satan:

1. Following his initial rebellion against God, he was cast from his original position of privilege in heaven (Ezekiel 28:16).
2. He was judged in the Garden of Eden after leading Adam and Eve into sin (Genesis 3:14-15).
3. He was judged at the cross (John 12:31; see also Colossians 2:15; Hebrews 2:14).[26] "Christ partook of

humanity, and through His substitutionary death He defeated Satan, rendering him impotent in the believer's life."[27]

4. He will be cast out of heaven in the middle of the seven-year tribulation period (Revelation 12:13). During this time he will be barred from all access to heaven.
5. He will be confined in "the Abyss" during the future 1000-year millennial kingdom over which Christ will rule (Revelation 20:2).
6. He will be cast into the lake of fire at the end of the millennial kingdom, where he will dwell for the rest of eternity (Revelation 20:10; see also Matthew 25:41).

These passages show that even though Satan is presently active in our world, he is a judged being and is destined for eternal suffering. The execution of these judgments is not yet complete, but the judgments have been pronounced, and it's just a matter of time before Satan's final doom is brought about.

The World of Demons

What about the demons (or "hell's angels")? Where did they come from? Does the Bible refer to the fall of numerous angels who became demons? Scripture gives some hints that help us answer these questions.

Many scholars believe the first five verses of Revelation 12 contain a minihistory of Satan. In keeping with this, Revelation 12:4 seems to refer to the fall of the angels who followed Satan: "His [Satan's] tail swept a third of the stars out of the sky and flung them to the earth."[28] Commentators have long recognized that the Bible sometimes uses the word *stars* for angels (see Job 38:7). If *stars* refers to angels in Revelation 12:4, it would appear that after Lucifer rebelled against God, he was able to draw a third of the angelic realm after him. When he sinned, he did not sin alone but apparently led a massive angelic revolt against God.

Just a few verses later, we read of the "dragon and his angels" (Revelation 12:7; see also Ephesians 3:10; 6:12). Demons are undoubtedly fallen angels.[29] Elsewhere in the Bible, Satan (himself a fallen angel) is called "the prince of demons" (Matthew 12:24). Demons are Satan's emissaries; they promote his purpose to thwart the plan of God. They are highly committed to their dark prince, Satan.

> These spirits, having [made] an irrevocable choice to follow Satan, instead of remaining loyal to their Creator, have become irretrievably confirmed in wickedness, and irreparably abandoned to delusion. Hence, they are in full sympathy with their prince, and render him willing service in their varied ranks and positions of service in his highly organized kingdom of evil.[30]

Scripture portrays demons as evil and wicked. They are "unclean spirits" (Matthew 10:1 KJV), "evil spirits" (Luke 7:21), and "spiritual forces of evil" (Ephesians 6:12). All these terms point to the immoral nature of demons. It is not surprising, then, that many people involved in the occult are also involved in immorality.[31]

What kinds of wicked things do demons do? Among many other things, Scripture says they inflict physical diseases on people (such as speechlessness, Matthew 9:33; blindness, 12:22; and epilepsy, 17:15-18). They also afflict people with mental disorders (Mark 5:4-5; 9:20-22; Luke 8:27-29; 9:37-42). They cause people to be self-destructive (Mark 5:5; Luke 9:42). They are even responsible for the deaths of some people (Revelation 9:14-19).

Of course, we must be careful to note that even though demons can cause physical illnesses, Scripture distinguishes between natural illnesses and those that are demon-caused (Matthew 4:24; Mark 1:32; Luke 7:21; 9:1; Acts 5:16). Theologian Millard J. Erickson notes that in the case of numerous healings by Jesus, "no mention is made of demons. In Matthew, for example, no mention is made of demon exorcism in the case of the healing of the centurion's servant (8:5-13), the woman with the hemorrhage of twelve years' duration (9:19-20), the two blind men (9:27-30), the man with the withered hand (12:9-14), and those who touched the fringe of Jesus' garment (14:35-36)."[32] Therefore, we must not presume we are being afflicted by a demon every time we get sick.

Presently there are two classes or groups of demons: One group is free and active in opposing God and His people (Ephesians 2:1-3); the other group is confined. Charles Ryrie notes that "of those who are confined, some are temporarily so, while others are permanently confined in Tartarus (2 Peter 2:4 and Jude 6). The Greeks thought of Tartarus as a place of punishment lower than Hades. Those temporarily confined are in the abyss (Luke 8:31; Revelation 9:1-3,11), some apparently consigned there to await final judgment, while others will be loosed to be active on the earth [during the seven-year tribulation] (verses 1-3,11,14; 16:14)."[33]

Why are some fallen angels permanently confined? They are probably being punished for some sin other than the original rebellion against God. Some theologians believe these angels are guilty of the unnatural sin mentioned in Genesis 6:2-4, and because of the gross depravity of this sin, they are permanently confined to Tartarus.[34]

Ranks Among Fallen Angels

Earlier in the book we saw that the angels are organized according to rank. The same is true among the fallen angels (Ephesians 6:12). Their ranks include principalities, powers, rulers of the darkness of this world, and spiritual wickedness in high places.[35] And all fallen angels, regardless of their individual ranks, follow the leadership of their malevolent commander in chief, Satan, the prince of demons.

The high degree of organization in the kingdom of darkness may sometimes make Satan appear to be omniscient or omnipotent. Demons report to Satan from all over the world, thereby extending his own reach and influence. But as we noted earlier, Satan is neither omniscient nor omnipotent. He is a creature with creaturely limitations. Tony Evans makes this comment:

> There is this common idea afloat that God and Satan are archrivals on more or less the same footing, battling to see who will be the ultimate victor...But nothing could be further from the truth. Satan's counterpart in the spiritual realm is the archangel Michael, not God. God has no counterpart. God is the Creator; Satan is His creation—who was created good but chose to rebel. God is all-knowing, all-powerful, and all-present. Satan has none of these attributes.[36]

Varying Degrees of Depravity

Scriptures hints at varying degrees of depravity among the fallen angels. Jesus spoke of a demon who left his abode but then returned, bringing with him "seven other spirits more wicked than [him]self" (Matthew 12:45). Clearly then, Jesus indicates that some demons are more evil than others. This seems to be in line with the teaching that some demons have committed acts so depraved that they are presently imprisoned (2 Peter 2:4).

Fallen Angels and Unbelievers

Second Corinthians 4:4 says that Satan blinds the minds of unbelievers to the truth of the gospel. This passage indicates that Satan inhibits the unbeliever's ability to think or reason properly in regard to spiritual matters.[37] One of the ways Satan does this is by leading people to think that any way to heaven is as acceptable as another. In other words, Satan promotes the idea that a person doesn't need to believe in Jesus Christ as the only means to salvation.

Satan also seeks to snatch the Word of God from the hearts of unbelievers when they hear it (Luke 8:12). Demons, under Satan's lead, work to disperse false doctrine (1 Timothy 4:1). As well, they wield influence over false prophets (1 John 4:1-4) and try to turn men to the worship of idols (see Leviticus 17:7; Deuteronomy 32:17; Psalm 106:36-38). In short, fallen angels do all they can to spread spiritual deception.

Fallen Angels and Believers

Fallen angels actively seek to harm believers in various ways.

- Satan tempts believers to sin (Ephesians 2:1-3; 1 Thessalonians 3:5).
- Satan tempts believers to lie (Acts 5:3).
- Satan tempts believers to commit sexually immoral acts (1 Corinthians 7:5).
- Satan accuses and slanders believers (Revelation 12:10).

- Satan hinders the work of believers in any way he can (1 Thessalonians 2:18).
- Satan and his demons wage war against and try to defeat believers (Ephesians 6:11-12).
- Satan sows tares among believers (Matthew 13:38-39).
- Satan incites persecutions against believers (Revelation 2:10).
- Satan opposes Christians with the ferociousness of a hungry lion (1 Peter 5:8).
- Satan plants doubt in the minds of believers (Genesis 3:1-5).
- Satan seeks to foster spiritual pride in the hearts of Christians (1 Timothy 3:6).
- Satan attempts to lead believers away from "the simplicity and purity of devotion to Christ" (2 Corinthians 11:3 NASB).
- Demons hinder answers to the prayers of believers (Daniel 10:12-20).
- Demons endeavor to instigate jealousy and faction among believers (James 3:13-16).
- Demons would separate the believer from Christ if they could (Romans 8:38-39).
- Demons cooperate with Satan in working against believers (Matthew 25:41; Ephesians 6:12; Revelation 12:7-12).

What About Demon Possession?

Charles Ryrie defines demon possession this way:

> A demon residing in a person, exerting direct control and influence over that person, with certain derangement of mind and/or body. Demon possession is to be distinguished from demon influence or demon activity in relation to a person. The work of the demon in the latter is from the outside; in demon possession it is from within.[38]

A person who is demon possessed may manifest unusual, superhuman strength (Mark 5:2-4). He may act in bizarre ways, such as going nude and living among tombs rather than in a house (Luke 8:27). The possessed person often engages in self-destructive behavior (Matthew 17:15; Mark 5:5).[39] These are just a few of the biblical signs of demon possession.

Ryrie says that according to his definition above, a Christian cannot be possessed by a demon because he is indwelt by the Holy Spirit.[40] I believe Ryrie is right. Because the Holy Spirit perpetually indwells Christians (1 Corinthians 6:19), they cannot be demon possessed. I like the way Walter Martin put it: When the devil knocks on the door of the Christian's heart, the Holy Spirit opens it and says, "Get lost!"

The Scriptures do not include a single instance of a Christian being demon possessed. For sure, Christians are afflicted by the devil, but they are not possessed by him.

God's Word clearly states that Christians have been delivered from Satan's domain. As Colossians 1:13 says, "He has rescued us from the dominion of darkness and brought us into the kingdom of the Son he loves." In addition, we must remember that "the one who is in you is greater than the one who is in the world" (1 John 4:4). This statement would not make much sense if Christians could be possessed by the devil.

Having said this, however, we must acknowledge that

even though a Christian cannot be possessed, he can still be oppressed or influenced by demonic powers. But the oppression or influence is external to the Christian, not internal. The demons work from outside the Christian to hinder him; they do not work from within him.[41]

The Christian's Defense

We Christians should be thankful that God has made provision for our defense against Satan and his fallen angels. What does this defense consist of?

To begin, we must ever keep in mind that twice the New Testament tells us that the Lord Jesus lives in heaven to make intercession for us (Romans 8:34; Hebrews 7:25). In other words, Jesus prays for us on a regular basis. Certainly His intercession for us includes the kind of intercession He made for His disciples in John 17:15, where He asked the Father to keep them safe from the evil one.

Beyond this, God has provided us with spiritual armor for our defense (Ephesians 6:11-18). Each piece of armor is important and serves its own special purpose. But you and I must choose to put on this armor. God doesn't force us to dress in it. We do it by choice. Read Paul's description of this armor:

> Put on the full armor of God so that you can take your stand against the devil's schemes.
>
> For our struggle is not against flesh and blood, but against the rulers, against the authorities, against the powers of this dark world and against the spiritual forces of evil in the heavenly realms.
>
> Therefore put on the full armor of God, so that when the day of evil comes, you may be able to stand

> your ground, and after you have done everything, to stand.
>
> Stand firm then, with the belt of truth buckled around your waist, with the breastplate of righteousness in place, and with your feet fitted with the readiness that comes from the gospel of peace.
>
> In addition to all this, take up the shield of faith, with which you can extinguish all the flaming arrows of the evil one.
>
> Take the helmet of salvation and the sword of the Spirit, which is the word of God.
>
> And pray in the Spirit on all occasions with all kinds of prayers and requests.
>
> With this in mind, be alert and always keep on praying for all the saints.

Without wearing this spiritual armor, you and I don't stand a chance against the forces of darkness. But with the armor on, victory is ours. Wearing this armor means that our lives will be characterized by such things as righteousness, obedience to the will of God, faith in God, and an effective use of the Word of God. These spell defeat for the devil. In effect, putting on the armor of God amounts to putting on Jesus Christ—who Himself defeated the devil (Matthew 4:3-11; Acts 10:38). (Good books are available that fully explain how to put on this spiritual armor.)[42]

Effective use of the Word of God is especially important for spiritual victory. Jesus used the Word to defeat the devil during His wilderness temptations (Matthew 4). We must learn to do the same.

> Obviously, the greater exposure there is to Scripture the more the Spirit can use this mighty sword in our lives. If you never read or study your Bible, you are terribly exposed to defeat and despair. You have no defense; you have nothing to put up against these forces that are at work. Therefore, learn to read your Bible regularly.[43]

Scripture specifically instructs us that each believer must be informed and thereby alert to the attacks of Satan (1 Peter 5:8). A prerequisite to defeating an enemy is to know as much as you can about him—including his tactics. The apostle Paul says, "We are not [to be] ignorant of his schemes" (2 Corinthians 2:11). We find all the information we need about this enemy and his schemes in the Word of God.

We are instructed to take a decisive stand against Satan. James 4:7 says, "Resist the devil, and he will flee from you." This is not a one-time resistance. Rather, we must steadfastly resist the devil on a day-to-day basis. When we do, he will flee from us. Similarly, Ephesians 6:13-14 tells us to "stand firm" against the devil. We do this not in our own strength but in the strength of Christ. After all, Christ "disarmed the rulers and authorities…[and] made a public display of them, having triumphed over them" (Colossians 2:15).

We must not give place to the devil by letting "the sun go down while you are still angry" toward someone (Ephesians 4:27). Permitting unrighteous anger to dwell in our heart gives opportunity to the devil to work in our lives.

We are instructed to rely on the indwelling Spirit of God, remembering that "the one who is in you is greater than the one who is in the world" (1 John 4:4).

We should pray for ourselves and for each other. Jesus set

an example for us in the Lord's Prayer by teaching us to pray, "Deliver us from the evil one" (Matthew 6:13). This should be a daily prayer. Jesus also set an example of how to pray for others in His prayer for Peter: "Simon, Simon, Satan has asked to sift you as wheat. But I have prayed for you, Simon, that your faith may not fail" (Luke 22:31-32). We should pray for each other that we will maintain a strong faith in the face of adversity.

Of course, the believer should never dabble in the occult, for this gives the devil opportunity to work in our lives (Deuteronomy 18:10-11; see also Romans 16:19).

Finally, we must remember that Satan is on a leash. He cannot go beyond what God will allow him (the book of Job makes this abundantly clear).[44] Thus, we should rest secure in the fact that God is in control of the universe and realize that Satan cannot simply do as he pleases in our lives.

The Key to Victory

By following these disciplines, we will have victory over Satan and his host of demons. And above all, remember that successfully defeating the powers of darkness rests not on what you can do in your own strength but on what Christ has already done. Indeed, you are more than a conqueror through Him who loved us (Romans 8:37)!

PART 4

Our Future with the Angels

I thank thee, O Lord, that Thou hast so set eternity within my heart that no earthly thing can ever satisfy me wholly.

~ John Baillie (1741–1806) ~

16

Anticipating Eternity

The light in which our glorious God dwells is superior to all things visible.

> It is something other than the radiance of all suns and stars. It is not to be beheld by earthly eyes; it is "unapproachable" (1 Timothy 6:16), far removed from all things this side (2 Corinthians 12:4). Only the angels in heaven can behold it (Matthew 18:10); only the spirits of the perfected in the eternal light (Matthew 5:8; 1 John 3:2; Revelation 22:4); only the pure and holy, even as He Himself is pure (1 John 3:2-3).[1]

One day, we as Christians will dwell with Christ face-to-face in His unveiled, glorious presence. When we receive our glorified resurrection bodies, the perishable will have become imperishable and the mortal will have become immortal (1 Corinthians 15:50-53). In our present bodies, we cannot endure in the direct presence of the triune God (His glory is too great, too overwhelming), but our resurrection bodies will be specially suited to dwelling in His presence.

Scripture tells us that even now, Christ is preparing an eternal, glorious dwelling place for us (John 14:1-3). If the present created universe with its incredible starry host is any indication of what Christ can do (John 1:3; Colossians 1:16; Hebrews 1:2,10), then this eternal dwelling place must be truly astounding (see 1 Corinthians 2:9).

When we enter into glory, we will be able to perceive angels just as clearly as you and I perceive each other here on earth (1 Corinthians 13:12). We will see them just as clearly as they see us. And we will jointly serve our glorious King—Jesus Christ—from eternity to eternity, from age to age forevermore.

Meanwhile, as David Jeremiah notes, "Just thinking about angels can give us a fresh reminder that there's another world besides this one that clings so closely all round us. Angels already experience the fullness of that other world—God's eternal, heavenly kingdom—where God's rule goes entirely unopposed and unquestioned. Someday we'll experience it with them."[2]

Joining the Angels' Song

One day, the voices of the saved will be joined with the voices of the angels in worship and praise to our eternal God. The book of Revelation describes this glorious scene in detail:

> After this I looked and there before me was a great multitude that no one could count, from every nation, tribe, people and language, standing before the throne and in front of the Lamb.
>
> They were wearing white robes and were holding palm branches in their hands.
>
> And they cried out in a loud voice: "Salvation belongs to our God, who sits on the throne, and to the Lamb."

> All the angels were standing around the throne and around the elders and the four living creatures.
>
> They fell down on their faces before the throne and worshiped God, saying: "Amen! Praise and glory and wisdom and thanks and honor and power and strength be to our God forever and ever. Amen!" (Revelation 7:9-12).

Imagine what this will be like—more than 100 million angels and untold millions of the redeemed singing praises to God in unity and harmony. I shiver just to hear a good human choir of a few dozen people sing a great anthem. But to have hundreds of millions of angels and believers singing in unison…incredible!

Focusing on God Alone

God's provision of angels should bring consolation to us during our earthly sojourns as we make our way to the heavenly city (Hebrews 11:16). We can rejoice that God's holy angels encamp around us, defending us day and night from unseen enemies and unapprehended dangers. However, we must never let a fascination with angels come between us and God. We are not to look to the angels for our refuge, nor are we to invoke their aid. God is our refuge, and we are to invoke His aid—and at His prerogative, the angels will render assistance as He directs.

In Scripture, God is always on center stage, and the angels exist solely to do His bidding. They never act independently of God.

As Christians, let's resolve to be perpetually excited at God's provisions for us (including the angels), yet at the same time may our eyes ever remain focused on our beloved Christ. Let's not become distracted so that we turn away from our first love. Christ is supreme!

Facing Adversity

Keeping our eyes focused on Christ is especially important when life throws us a punch (John 16:33). If something bad should happen to you (such as a car wreck), you may be tempted to ask, "Where was my angel?" Hope MacDonald gives us the right perspective with these words:

> We must recognize the fact that every person, at one time or another, will face sickness, heartache, suffering, and death. We remember that our faith and trust is not in a visible angel or in some miraculous deliverance, but in God alone. We rest in the knowledge that God may not always be understood, but He can *always* be trusted.[3]

We do well to keep in mind that God sometimes uses adversities in our lives to develop our faith muscles and to make us strong, mature believers. And even though God may not always remove us from the midst of adversity, He will always walk with us through it (Psalm 23:4).

If the time ever comes when we witness a visible appearance of one of God's glorious angels, it will be all the sweeter simply because we have learned to trust in Christ without depending on such supernatural occurrences. We have learned from experience that Christ alone is worthy of our confidence.

Looking Toward Eternity

As we continue to keep Christ supreme in our hearts, we can ponder the greatness of what lies ahead. As Scripture tells us, "No eye has seen, no ear has heard, no mind has conceived what God has prepared for those who love him" (1 Corinthians 2:9).

The apostle John describes our eternal destiny this way:

I saw a new heaven and a new earth, for the first heaven and the first earth had passed away, and there was no longer any sea.

I saw the Holy City, the new Jerusalem, coming down out of heaven from God, prepared as a bride beautifully dressed for her husband.

And I heard a loud voice from the throne saying, "Now the dwelling of God is with men, and he will live with them. They will be his people, and God himself will be with them and be their God. He will wipe every tear from their eyes. There will be no more death or mourning or crying or pain, for the old order of things has passed away."

He who was seated on the throne said, "I am making everything new!" Then he said, "Write this down, for these words are trustworthy and true" (Revelation 21:1-5).

Amen!

Notes

From the Voices of Angels

1. Craig S. Keener, *The IVP Bible Background Commentary* (Downers Grove, IL: InterVarsity, 1993), p. 779.
2. John MacArthur, *The Glory of Heaven: The Truth About Heaven, Angels, and Eternal Life* (Wheaton, IL: Crossway, 1996), p. 161.

Chapter 1—Angels in the World Today

Epigraph. Cited in Edythe Draper, ed., *Draper's Book of Quotations for the Christian World* (Grand Rapids: Baker Books, 1992), p. 386.

1. I have changed people's names and some details of their situation to protect their privacy.
2. Billy Graham, *Angels: God's Secret Agents* (Garden City, NY: Doubleday, 1975), p. 152.
3. Cited in Timothy Jones, "Rumors of Angels: Telling Fact from Fad," *Christianity Today,* April 5, 1993, p. 22.
4. Cited in Graham, *Angels,* p. 3.
5. Corrie ten Boom, *Marching Orders for the End Battle* (Fort Washington, PA: Christian Literature Crusade, 1969), pp. 89-90. The story is cited in Joan Wester Anderson, *Where Angels Walk* (New York: Ballantine, 1992), pp. 159-60.
6. Cited in Duane A. Garrett, *Angels and the New Spirituality* (Nashville: Broadman and Holman, 1995), pp. 179-80.
7. Cited in Dawn Raffel, "Angels All Around Us: More and More People Claim They've Seen or Felt These Heavenly Messengers," *Redbook,* December 1992, p. 82.
8. Cited in L.W. Northrup, *Encounters with Angels* (Wheaton: Tyndale House, 1993), p. 38.
9. A.C. Gaebelein, *What the Bible Says About Angels* (Grand Rapids: Baker Books, 1993), p. 99.

10. "Angel Lore: Real-Life Encounters with Angels," *Ladies Home Journal,* December 1993, p. 192.
11. Ray C. Stedman, *Hebrews* (Downers Grove, IL: InterVarsity, 1992), p. 31.

Chapter 2—Flying High: The Popularity of Angels

Epigraph. Laura Davis, "Is Your Guardian Angel Waiting in the Wings?" *Daily Post* (Liverpool), September 22, 2004.

1. Cecelia Goodnow, "An Angel on Your Shoulder: More Mortals Are Getting a Boost from the Beyond," *San Francisco Examiner,* August 25, 1993, p. C7.
2. Carl Herko, "Angels: Flying High from Newsletters to Pop Music—It's a Trend for Our Times," *Buffalo News,* January 8, 1993, p. G18.
3. Nancy Gibbs, "Angels Among Us," *Time,* December 29, 1993.
4. Kenneth L. Woodward, "Angels: Hark! America's Latest Search for Spiritual Meaning Has a Halo Effect," *Newsweek,* December 27, 1993, pp. 52-53.
5. Dawn Raffel, "Angels All Around Us: More and More People Claim They've Seen or Felt These Heavenly Messengers," *Redbook,* December 1992, p. 82.
6. Burt Constable, "Hark!" *Chicago Daily Herald,* August 13, 2005.
7. Kevin Eckstrom, "Poll: Belief in Angels, Devil on the Rise," *Religion News Service,* May 26, 2004.
8. Dana Blanton, "Fox Poll: More Believe in Heaven than Hell," Fox News, October 28, 2005.
9. "Americans Believe in Angels, Poll Says," Associated Press, December 23, 2006.
10. Terry Lynn Taylor, *Answers from the Angels: A Book of Angel Letters* (Tiburon, CA: Kramer, 1993), p. 89; Terry Lynn Taylor, *Messengers of Light: The Angels' Guide to Spiritual Growth* (Tiburon, CA: Kramer, 1990), pp. xx, 19; Terry Lynn Taylor, *Messengers of Love, Light and Grace* (Novato, CA: Kramer, 2005), pp. 12, 35, 229.
11. Timothy Jones, "Rumors of Angels: Telling Fact from Fad," *Christianity Today,* April 5, 1993, p. 20; Taylor, *Messengers of Love, Light, and Grace,* p. 243; Gibbs, "Angels Among Us"; Susan Hall-Balduf, "Angel Aware: Graceful Stories from Heavens Afar," *Detroit Free Press,* December 15, 1993, p. 3E; Goodnow, "An Angel on Your Shoulder"; Sophy Burnham, *A Book of Angels* (New York: Random House, 2004), p. 122; Woodward, "Angels," pp. 54-55.
12. Burnham, *A Book of Angels,* pp. 279-81; Taylor, *Messengers of Love, Light, and Grace,* p. 44.
13. Joan Wester Anderson, *Guardian Angels: True Stories of Answered Prayers* (Chicago: Loyola Press, 2006), p. 146.

14. Terry Lynn Taylor and Mary Beth Crain, *Angel Courage: 365 Meditations and Insights to Get Us Through Hard Times* (New York: HarperCollins, 1999), q.v. February 22.
15. Taylor, *Messengers of Love, Light, and Grace,* pp. 8-9; Paul D. Williams, *What the World Needs Now: Healing Messages from Angels* (Victoria, BC: Trafford Publishing, 2003), p. 122.
16. Richard Scheinin, "Look Earthward Angel," *San Jose Mercury News,* June 5, 1993, p. 1C; see also Taylor, *Messengers of Love, Light, and Grace,* pp. 43, 98; Eileen Elias Freeman, *Touched by Angels* (New York: Warner, 1993), p. xiii.
17. Lisa Daniels, "Faithful Are Aflutter," *San Jose Mercury News,* November 26, 1992, p. 18H; see also Joan Wester Anderson, *In the Arms of Angels: True Stories of Heavenly Guardians* (Chicago: Loyola Press, 2004), pp. 96, 140, 195.
18. "An Age for Angels," Associated Press, p. 4.
19. David Jeremiah, *What the Bible Says About Angels* (Sisters, OR: Multnomah, 1996), p. 15; see also Burnham, *A Book of Angels,* p. 194; Taylor, *Messengers of Love, Light, and Grace,* p. 8.
20. Eckstrom, "Poll: Belief in Angels, Devil on the Rise," *Religion News Service.*
21. Taylor and Crain, *Angel Courage,* q.v. May 31.

Chapter 3—Celestial Quackery, Part 1

Epigraph. Terry Lynn Taylor, *Messengers of Love, Light, and Grace* (Novato, CA: Kramer, 2005), pp. 117-18.

1. Terry Lynn Taylor, *Messengers of Light: The Angels' Guide to Spiritual Growth* (Tiburon, CA: Kramer, 1990), p. 9.
2. Taylor, *Messengers of Love, Light, and Grace,* pp. 4, 18.
3. Alma Daniel, Timothy Wyllie, and Andrew Ramer, *Ask Your Angels* (New York: Ballantine, 1992), pp. 3, 110, 124-25, 157.
4. Jane M. Howard, *Commune with the Angels* (Virginia Beach: A.R.E. Press, 1992), p. 28.
5. Sophy Burnham, *A Book of Angels* (New York: Random House, 2004), pp. xx, 52.
6. For a biblical response to channeling, visualization, the use of crystals, and other New Age concepts, see my book *The New Age Movement* (Grand Rapids: Zondervan, 1994).
7. John Ronner, *Do You Have a Guardian Angel?* (Murfreesboro, TN: Mamre Press, 1993), p. 106.
8. Howard, *Commune with the Angels,* p. 58.
9. Ibid.

10. Daniel, Wyllie, and Ramer, *Ask Your Angels,* p. 173.
11. Timothy Jones, "Rumors of Angels: Telling Fact from Fad," *Christianity Today,* April 5, 1993, p. 19.
12. Alice Johnson, "Contacting Your Guardian Angel," *Longmont Daily Times,* May 2–3, 1981, p. 3.
13. Ibid.
14. John Edward, *Understanding Your Angels,* Audio CD (Carlsbad, CA: Hay House, 2003); John Edward, *What If God Were the Sun?* (New York: Princess Books, 2004), pp. 78-79, 94, 112.
15. James van Praagh, *Talking to Heaven: A Medium's Message of Life After Death* (New York: Signet, 1999), pp. 62-63, 94, 118; James van Praagh, *Heaven and Earth: Making the Psychic Connection* (New York: Pocket, 2006), pp. 66-67, 86, 98, 119, 141, 149, 200; James van Praagh, *Meditations with James Van Praagh* (New York: Fireside, 2003), p. 143.
16. Sylvia Brown, *Spiritual Connections: How to Find Spirituality Throughout All the Relationships in Your Life* (Carlsbad, CA: Hay House, 2007), pp. 30, 32, 67, 70-71, 79, 83, 87-88; Sylvia Browne and Lindsay Harrison, *Phenomenon: Everything You Need to Know About the Paranormal* (New York: NAL Trade, 2006), pp. 51, 62, 75-76, 163-65, 289; Sylvia Browne and Lindsay Harrison, *Life on the Other Side: A Psychic's Tour of the Afterlife* (New York: NAL Trade, 2002), pp. 32-33, 40, 63-64, 99, 151-56.
17. Taylor, *Messengers of Love, Light, and Grace,* p. 109.
18. John Edward, *One Last Time: A Psychic Medium Speaks to Those We Have Loved and Lost* (New York: Berkley Books, 1999), p. 43.
19. "John Edward Is the Oprah of the Other Side," *New York Times Magazine,* July 29, 2001.
20. Terry Lynn Taylor, *Answers from the Angels: A Book of Angel Letters* (Tiburon, CA: Kramer, 1993), p. 39.
21. The editors of Beliefnet, *The Big Book of Angels: Angelic Encounters, Expert Answers, Listening to and Working with Your Angels* (Emmaus, PA: Rodale, 2002), p. 17.
22. Taylor, *Messengers of Light,* pp. 110-11.
23. Taylor, *Messengers of Love, Light, and Grace,* p. 109.
24. Claire Nahmad, *Summoning Angels: How to Call on Angels in Every Life Situation* (New York: Sterling Publishing, 2004), p. 48; Terry Lynn Taylor and Mary Beth Crain, *Angel Courage: 365 Meditations and Insights to Get Us Through Hard Times* (New York: HarperCollins, 1999), q.v. March 21.
25. Rekha Vidyarthi, *Emotional Healing with Angels: A Spiritual Guide to Knowing, Healing, and Freeing Your True Self* (Victoria, BC: Trafford Publishing, 2005), p. 40.

26. Taylor, *Messengers of Love, Light, and Grace,* p. 19.
27. Howard, *Commune with the Angels,* p. 81; see also Taylor, *Messengers of Love, Light, and Grace,* p. 148.
28. Taylor, *Messengers of Light,* p. 108.
29. Taylor, *Messengers of Love, Light, and Grace,* pp. 115-16.
30. Taylor, *Messengers of Love, Light, and Grace,* pp. 8-9; Paul D. Williams, *What the World Needs Now: Healing Messages from Angels* (Victoria, BC: Trafford Publishing, 2003), p. 122.
31. Robert C. Smith, *In the Presence of Angels: Stories from New Research on Angelic Influences* (Virginia Beach: A.R.E. Press, 1993), p. 74.
32. Howard, *Commune with the Angels,* p. 50.
33. Taylor, *Messengers of Love, Light, and Grace,* p. 109.
34. Daniel, Wyllie, and Ramer, *Ask Your Angels,* p. 237.
35. Ibid.
36. Taylor, *Messengers of Light,* p. 71.
37. Daniel, Wyllie, and Ramer, *Ask Your Angels,* p. 239.
38. Taylor, *Messengers of Love, Light, and Grace,* pp. 117-18.
39. Daniel, Wyllie, and Ramer, *Ask Your Angels,* pp. 239-40.
40. The editors of BeliefNet, *The Big Book of Angels,* p. 211; Christine Astell, *Discovering Angels: Wisdom, Healing, Destiny* (New York: Sterling Publishing, 2005), p. 153; Terah Cox, *Birth Angels: Fulfilling Your Life Purpose with the 72 Angels of the Kabbalah* (Riverside, NJ: Andrews McMeel Publishing, 2004), p. 113.
41. Kenneth L. Woodward, "Angels: Hark! America's Latest Search for Spiritual Meaning Has a Halo Effect," *Newsweek,* December 27, 1993, p. 55.
42. Howard, *Commune with the Angels,* p. 58.

Chapter 4—Celestial Quackery, Part 2

Epigraph. Sophy Burnham, *A Book of Angels* (New York: Random House, 2004), p. xxv.

1. Laura Davis, "Is Your Guardian Angel Waiting in the Wings?" *Daily Post* (Liverpool), September 22, 2004.
2. Marilyn Achiron, "The Halo Effect," *People Weekly,* May 17, 1993, p. 75; Cecelia Goodnow, "An Angel on Your Shoulder," *San Francisco Examiner,* August 25, 1993, p. C7; Pythia Peay, "The Presence of Angels," *Common Boundary,* January–February 1991, p. 30.
3. Eileen Elias Freeman, *Touched by Angels* (New York: Warner, 1993), p. 71.

4. Achiron, "The Halo Effect," p. 75.
5. John Ronner, *Do You Have a Guardian Angel?* (Murfreesboro, TN: Mamre Press, 1993), p. 110.
6. Terry Lynn Taylor, *Messengers of Love, Light, and Grace* (Novato, CA: Kramer, 2005), p. 13.
7. Jane M. Howard, *Commune with the Angels* (Virginia Beach: A.R.E. Press, 1992), p. 11.
8. Taylor, *Messengers of Love, Light, and Grace,* p. 13.
9. Burnham, *A Book of Angels,* pp. xxv, 114; see also Nancy Gibbs, "Angels Among Us," *Time,* December 29, 1993.
10. Peay, "The Presence of Angels," p. 30.
11. Taylor, *Messengers of Love, Light, and Grace,* pp. 8-9, 47.
12. Terry Lynn Taylor and Mary Beth Crain, *Angel Courage: 365 Meditations and Insights to Get Us Through Hard Times* (New York: HarperCollins, 1999), q.v. April 8.
13. Taylor, *Messengers of Love, Light, and Grace,* pp. 138-39; see also pp. 242-43.
14. Burnham, *A Book of Angels,* pp. 36, 313; Peay, "The Presence of Angels," p. 30; Daniel, Wyllie, and Ramer, *Ask Your Angels,* p. 174; Taylor, *Messengers of Love, Light, and Grace,* p. 100.
15. Terry Lynn Taylor, *Messengers of Light: The Angels' Guide to Spiritual Growth* (Tiburon, CA: Kramer, 1990), pp. 6, 16, 18-19, 21-22, 80, 148; see also Taylor, *Messengers of Love, Light and Grace,* pp. 30-32, 50, 58, 66, 86.
16. Daniel, Wyllie, and Ramer, *Ask Your Angels,* p. 4.
17. Taylor, *Messengers of Light,* p. 99; see also Taylor, *Messengers of Love, Light, and Grace,* p. 120; Howard, *Commune with the Angels,* pp. 81-82.
18. Taylor, *Messengers of Light,* p. 78; Taylor, *Messengers of Love, Light, and Grace,* p. 123.
19. Freeman, *Touched by Angels,* p. xiv.
20. Taylor, *Messengers of Love, Light, and Grace,* pp. 121-22.
21. Ibid., p. 31.
22. Sophy Burnham, *Angel Letters* (New York: Ballantine, 1991), p. ix; see also Burnham, *A Book of Angels,* p. 37.
23. Taylor, *Messengers of Love, Light, and Grace,* p. 24.
24. Taylor, *Answers from the Angels,* p. 145.
25. Daniel, Wyllie, and Ramer, *Ask Your Angels,* pp. 300-301.

26. Ibid.
27. Freeman, *Touched by Angels,* p. 68.
28. Ibid., pp. 69-70.
29. Taylor, *Messengers of Light,* p. 31; see also Taylor and Crain, *Angel Courage,* q.v. June 2.
30. Taylor and Crain, *Angel Courage,* q.v. March 20, June 12, September 15; Taylor, *Messengers of Love, Light, and Grace,* p. 35.
31. Taylor, *Messengers of Love, Light, and Grace,* p. 20.
32. Terry Lynn Taylor, *Creating with the Angels,* (Tiburon, CA: H.J. Kramer, 1993), p. 37.
33. Joan Wester Anderson, *Guardian Angels: True Stories of Answered Prayers* (Chicago: Loyola Press, 2006), p. 146; Taylor, *Messengers of Love, Light, and Grace,* p. 63; Taylor and Crain, *Angel Courage,* q.v. February 22.
34. Taylor, *Messengers of Love, Light, and Grace,* p. 43.
35. John Calvin, *Institutes of the Christian Religion,* ed. John T. McNeill, trans. Ford Lewis Battles (Philadelphia: The Westminster Press, 1960), 1.14.4.
36. See Duane Garrett, *Angels and the New Spirituality* (Nashville: Broadman and Holman, 1995).
37. As claimed in Burnham, *A Book of Angels,* pp. 314-15.

Chapter 5—The Origin of Angels

1. Charles C. Ryrie, *Basic Theology* (Wheaton: Victor Books, 1986), p. 122.
2. Ryrie, *Basic Theology,* p. 122.
3. John Calvin, *Institutes of the Christian Religion,* ed. John T. McNeill, trans. Ford Lewis Battles (Philadelphia: Westminster Press, 1960), 1.14.4.
4. David Connolly, *In Search of Angels. A Celestial Sourcebook for Beginning Your Journey* (New York: Perigee Books, 1993), p. 69.
5. John C. Whitcomb, *The Early Earth* (Grand Rapids: Baker Books, 1983), pp. 24-25.
6. Louis Berkhof, *Systematic Theology* (Grand Rapids: Eerdmans, 1982), p. 146.
7. William H. Baker, "Our Chariots of Fire," *Moody Monthly,* January 1986, p. 35.
8. John Eadie, *A Commentary on the Greek Text of the Epistle of Paul to the Colossians* (Grand Rapids: Baker Books, 1979), p. 51.
9. See Marvin R. Vincent, *Word Studies in the New Testament,* vol. 3 (Grand Rapids: Eerdmans, 1975), pp. 469-70; Kenneth S. Wuest, *Wuest's Word Studies,* vol. 1 (Grand Rapids: Eerdmans, 1973), p. 184.

10. John MacArthur, *The Glory of Heaven: The Truth about Heaven, Angels, and Eternal Life* (Wheaton: Crossway, 1996), p. 152.

11. F.F. Bruce, ed., *The International Bible Commentary* (Grand Rapids: Zondervan, 1986), p. 1454.

12. Cited in Connolly, *In Search of Angels,* p. 69.

13. See Roy Zuck, *Job* (Chicago: Moody Press, 1978), pp. 15, 166; compare *The International Bible Commentary,* p. 546; and Charles F. Pfeiffer and Everett F. Harrison, eds., *The Wycliffe Bible Commentary* (Chicago: Moody Press, 1974), p. 461.

14. James Montgomery Boice, *Foundations of the Christian Faith* (Downers Grove, IL: InterVarsity, 1981), p. 167.

15. C. Fred Dickason, *Angels, Elect and Evil* (Chicago: Moody Press, 1978), p. 26.

16. Charles Hodge, *Systematic Theology,* abridged edition, ed. Edward N. Gross (Grand Rapids: Baker Books, 1988), p. 232.

17. Dickason, *Angels, Elect and Evil,* p. 26.

18. Ryrie, *Basic Theology,* p. 127.

19. Berkhof, *Systematic Theology,* p. 145.

20. Dickason, *Angels, Elect and Evil,* pp. 40-41.

21. Henry Clarence Thiessen, *Lectures in Systematic Theology* (Grand Rapids: Eerdmans, 1981), p. 134.

22. Lewis Sperry Chafer, *Systematic Theology,* abridged edition, ed. John F. Walvoord (Wheaton: Victor Books, 1989), p. 284.

Chapter 6—The Nature of Angels

Epigraph. Cited by Lisa Daniels, "Faithful Are Aflutter About Angels," *San Jose Mercury News,* November 26, 1992, p. 18H.

1. G.W. Bromiley, "Angels," in *Evangelical Dictionary of Theology,* ed. Walter A. Elwell (Grand Rapids: Baker Books, 1984), p. 46.

2. Cited in David Connolly, *In Search of Angels: A Celestial Sourcebook for Beginning Your Journey* (New York: Perigee Books, 1993), p. 17.

3. Henry Clarence Thiessen, *Lectures in Systematic Theology* (Grand Rapids: Eerdmans, 1981), p. 133.

4. C. Fred Dickason, *Angels, Elect and Evil* (Chicago: Moody Press, 1978), p. 56.

5. Duane A. Garrett, *Angels and the New Spirituality* (Nashville: Broadman and Holman, 1995), p. 103.

6. Louis Berkhof, *Manual of Christian Doctrine* (Grand Rapids: Eerdmans, 1983), p. 100.
7. Lewis Sperry Chafer and John F. Walvoord, *Major Bible Themes* (Grand Rapids: Zondervan, 1975), p. 152.
8. Charles C. Ryrie, *Basic Theology* (Wheaton: Victor Books, 1986), p. 126.
9. Augustus Hopkins Strong, *Systematic Theology* (Old Tappan, NJ: Revell, 1979), p. 445.
10. William H. Baker, "Our Chariots of Fire," *Moody Monthly,* January 1986, p. 35.
11. Billy Graham, *Angels: God's Secret Agents* (Garden City, NY: Doubleday, 1975), p. 24.
12. Ibid., p. 28.
13. Dickason, *Angels, Elect and Evil,* p. 33.
14. Millard J. Erickson, *Christian Theology* (Grand Rapids: Baker Books, 1987), p. 440.
15. Dickason, *Angels, Elect and Evil,* p. 39.
16. Graham, *Angels: God's Secret Agents,* p. 19.
17. Dickason, *Angels, Elect and Evil,* p. 35, 44.
18. Peter Kreeft, *Angels (and Demons): What Do We Really Know About Them?* (San Francisco: Ignatius Press, 2004), p. 79.
19. Herbert Lockyer, *All the Angels in the Bible* (Peabody, MA: Hendrickson, 1995), p. 8.
20. Strong, *Systematic Theology,* p. 445.
21. Cited in Herbert Lockyer, *All the Angels in the Bible* (Peabody, MA: Hendrickson, 1995), p. 169.
22. Ryrie, *Basic Theology,* p. 125.
23. Dickason, *Angels, Elect and Evil,* p. 34.
24. Baker, "Our Chariots of Fire," p. 35.
25. Ryrie, *Basic Theology,* p. 126.

Chapter 7—The Organization of Angels

Epigraph. A. Duane Litfin, "Evangelical Feminism: Why Traditionalists Reject It," *Bibliotheca Sacra,* July-September 1979, p. 267.

1. See David Connolly, *In Search of Angels: A Celestial Sourcebook for Beginning Your Journey* (New York: Perigee Books, 1993), p. 78; Kenneth L. Woodward,

"Angels: Hark! America's Latest Search for Spiritual Meaning Has a Halo Effect," *Newsweek,* December 27, 1993, p. 57.

2. Cited in Connolly, *In Search of Angels,* p. 77.
3. C. Fred Dickason, *Angels, Elect and Evil* (Chicago: Moody Press, 1978), p. 86.
4. Charles C. Ryrie, *Basic Theology* (Wheaton: Victor Books, 1986), p. 128.
5. Peter Kreeft, *Angels (and Demons): What Do We Really Know About Them?* (San Francisco: Ignatius Press, 2004), pp. 91, 93.
6. Billy Graham, *Angels: God's Secret Agents* (Garden City, NY: Doubleday, 1975), p. 40.
7. David Jeremiah, *What the Bible Says About Angels* (Sisters: Multnomah, 1996), p. 76.
8. See J.B. Lightfoot, *Saint Paul's Epistles to the Colossians and to Philemon* (Grand Rapids: Zondervan, 1959), p. 152.
9. Louis Berkhof, *Systematic Theology* (Grand Rapids: Eerdmans, 1982), p. 147.
10. John Calvin, *Institutes of the Christian Religion,* ed. John T. McNeill, trans. Ford Lewis Battles (Philadelphia: Westminster Press, 1960), 1.14.5; see also Lightfoot, *Saint Paul's Epistles to the Colossians and to Philemon,* p. 154.
11. T.K. Abbott, *The International Critical Commentary: The Epistles to the Ephesians and to the Colossians* (Edinburgh, Scotland: T&T Clark, 1979), p. 216.
12. See Lightfoot, *Saint Paul's Epistles to the Colossians and to Philemon,* p. 154.
13. Henry Clarence Thiessen, *Lectures in Systematic Theology* (Grand Rapids: Eerdmans, 1981), p. 140.
14. Lewis Sperry Chafer, *Systematic Theology,* abridged edition, ed. John F. Walvoord (Wheaton: Victor Books, 1989), p. 285.
15. Lightfoot, *Saint Paul's Epistles to the Colossians and to Philemon,* p. 153.
16. A.A. Hodges, *Outlines of Theology* (Grand Rapids: Zondervan, 1972), p. 251.
17. Ryrie, *Basic Theology,* p. 128.
18. Dickason, *Angels, Elect and Evil,* p. 68.
19. Geoffrey W. Bromiley, ed. *International Standard Bible Encyclopedia,* vol. 3 (Grand Rapids: Eerdmans, 1986), p. 347.
20. Clinton E. Arnold, *Powers of Darkness: Principalities and Powers in Paul's Letters* (Downers Grove, IL: InterVarsity, 1992), p. 63.
21. Berkhof, *Systematic Theology,* p. 147.

22. Tony Evans, *The Truth about Angels and Demons* (Chicago: Moody Press, 2005), p. 45.

23. James Montgomery Boice, *Foundations of the Christian Faith* (Downers Grove, IL: InterVarsity, 1981), p. 168.

24. Dickason, *Angels, Elect and Evil,* p. 67.

25. Ray Stedman, *Hebrews* (Downers Grove, IL: InterVarsity, 1992), p. 29.

26. Boice, *Foundations of the Christian Faith,* p. 168.

27. Charles Dyer, "Ezekiel," in *The Bible Knowledge Commentary,* Old Testament, eds. John F. Walvoord and Roy B. Zuck (Wheaton: Victor Books, 1985), p. 1228.

28. Rene Pache, *The Future Life* (Chicago: Moody Press, 1962), p. 102.

29. Dickason, *Angels, Elect and Evil,* p. 63.

30. Ibid., p. 65.

31. Ibid., p. 66.

32. Herbert Lockyer, *All the Angels in the Bible* (Peabody, MA: Hendrickson, 1995), p. 32.

33. Dickason, *Angels, Elect and Evil,* p. 65.

34. Hodges, *Outlines of Theology,* p. 250.

35. Dickason, *Angels, Elect and Evil,* p. 70.

36. Lockyer, *All the Angels in the Bible,* p. 29.

37. Colin Brown, ed., *The New International Dictionary of New Testament Theology* (Grand Rapids: Zondervan, 1979), s.v. "Gabriel."

38. Boice, *Foundations of the Christian Faith,* p. 168.

39. A.C. Gaebelein, *What the Bible Says About Angels* (Grand Rapids: Baker Books, 1993), p. 17.

40. Litfin, "Evangelical Feminism: Why Traditionalists Reject It," p. 267.

Chapter 8—The Titles of Angels

Epigraph. Henri Cazelles, "Name," in *Dictionary of Biblical Theology,* ed. Zavier Leon-Dufour (New York: Seabury Press, 1983), p. 377.

1. Henry Clarence Thiessen, *Lectures in Systematic Theology* (Grand Rapids: Eerdmans, 1981), p. 139.

2. Emery H. Bancroft, *Christian Theology* (Grand Rapids: Zondervan, 1976), p. 311.

3. James Oliver Buswell, *A Systematic Theology of the Christian Religion* (Grand Rapids: Zondervan, 1979), 1:105.
4. Charles C. Ryrie, *Basic Theology* (Wheaton: Victor Books, 1986), p. 248.
5. Benjamin B. Warfield, *The Person and Work of Christ* (Philadelphia: Presbyterian and Reformed, 1950), p. 77.
6. C.F. Keil and F. Delitzsch, *Commentary on the Old Testament,* vol. 6 (Grand Rapids: Eerdmans, 1986), pp. 273-78; see also Robert Jamieson, A.R. Fausset, and David Brown, *A Commentary—Critical, Experimental, and Practical—on the Old and New Testaments* (Grand Rapids: Eerdmans, 1973), p. 508.
7. See R. Laird Harris, "Proverbs," in *The Wycliffe Bible Commentary,* eds. Charles F. Pfeiffer and Everett F. Harrison (Chicago: Moody Press, 1974), p. 581.
8. Albert Barnes, *Notes on the New Testament* (Grand Rapids: Baker Books, 1977), p. 45.
9. Ray C. Stedman, *Hebrews* (Downers Grove, IL: InterVarsity, 1992), p. 31.
10. Barnes, *Notes on the New Testament,* p. 45-46.
11. Ibid., p. 47.
12. C. Fred Dickason, *Angels, Elect and Evil* (Chicago: Moody Press, 1978), p. 59.
13. John Calvin, *Institutes of the Christian Religion,* ed. John T. McNeill, trans. Ford Lewis Battles (Philadelphia: Westminster Press, 1960), 1.14.5.
14. David Jeremiah, *What the Bible Says About Angels* (Sisters: Multnomah, 1996), p. 65.
15. Dickason, *Angels, Elect and Evil,* p. 59.
16. Jeremiah, *What the Bible Says About Angels,* p. 65.
17. See F.F. Bruce, ed., *The International Bible Commentary* (Grand Rapids: Zondervan, 1986), p. 281.
18. Thiessen, *Lectures in Systematic Theology,* p. 139.
19. John F. Walvoord, *Daniel: The Key to Prophetic Revelation* (Chicago: Moody Press, 1981), p. 102; Jeremiah, *What the Bible Says About Angels,* p. 136.
20. Herbert Lockyer, *All the Angels in the Bible* (Peabody, MA: Hendrickson, 1995), p. 39.
21. Walvoord, *Daniel,* p. 102.

Chapter 9—The Angel of the Lord

Epigraph. John Calvin, *Institutes of the Christian Religion,* ed. John T. McNeill, trans. Ford Lewis Battles, vol. 1 (Philadelphia: Westminster Press, 1960), p. 133.

1. See R. Alan Cole, *Exodus: An Introduction and Commentary* (Downers Grove, IL: InterVarsity, 1973), p. 65.
2. Guy B. Funderburk notes, "[The Angel] was not restricted to executing a single order, but, like Jesus, He spoke with authority as though He were God Himself. Only the Logos, or some other manifest personification of God, would be able to do that." ("Angel," in *The Zondervan Pictorial Encyclopedia of the Bible,* ed. Merrill C. Tenney, vol. 1 [Grand Rapids: Zondervan, 1978], p. 163.)
3. See H.C. Leupold, *Exposition of Genesis,* vol. 1 (Grand Rapids: Baker Books, 1980), p. 503.
4. Ron Rhodes, *Christ Before the Manger: The Life and Times of the Preincarnate Christ* (Grand Rapids: Baker Books, 1992).
5. See C.F. Keil and Franz Delitzsch, "Zechariah," in *Biblical Commentary on the Old Testament* (Grand Rapids: Eerdmans, 1954), p. 235.
6. See Rhodes, *Christ Before the Manger,* p. 84.
7. John Walvoord notes, "As the Angel of Jehovah characteristically appears in bodily, usually human form, He could not be the Holy Spirit who does not appear bodily, except in the rare instance of appearing in the form of a dove at the baptism of Christ." (John Walvoord, *Jesus Christ Our Lord* [Chicago: Moody Press, 1980], p. 46.)
8. Walvoord, *Jesus Christ Our Lord,* p. 54.
9. Rhodes, *Christ Before the Manger,* p. 86.
10. Ibid., p. 87.
11. Ibid.
12. Norman Geisler, *To Understand the Bible Look for Jesus* (Grand Rapids: Baker Books, 1979), p. 67.
13. See Josh McDowell and Bart Larson, *Jesus: A Biblical Defense of His Deity* (San Bernardino, CA: Here's Life, 1983), p. 79.
14. Irenaeus, *Against Heresies* (4.10.1), cited in Walvoord, *Jesus Christ Our Lord,* p. 55.
15. *First Apology,* lxii; lxiii; compare with *Martyr's Dialogue with Trypho,* p. 59; see McDowell and Larson, *Jesus: A Biblical Defense of His Deity,* p. 79.
16. Tertullian, *Against Praxeas,* p. 16; see also Tertullian's *Against Marcion,* 2.27; cited in Walvoord, *Jesus Christ Our Lord,* p. 55.
17. See Richard Watson, *Theological Institutes,* 2 vols., 29th ed. (New York: Nelson and Philips, 1850), pp. 501-2.
18. Charles Hodge, *Systematic Theology,* abridged edition, ed. Edward N. Gross (Grand Rapids: Baker Books, 1988), p. 177.

19. Francis Brown, S.R. Driver, and Charles A. Briggs, *A Hebrew and English Lexicon of the Old Testament* (Oxford: Clarendon Press, 1980), p. 521. See also H. Bietenhard, *New Testament Theology,* ed. Colin Brown, vol. 1 (Grand Rapids: Zondervan, 1979), S.V. "angel."
20. Calvin, *Institutes of the Christian Religion,* p. 133.

Chapter 10—Celestial Spectators of Planet Earth

Epigraph. Rene Pache, *The Future Life* (Chicago: Moody Press, 1980), p. 116.

1. David Jeremiah, *What the Bible Says About Angels* (Sisters, OR: Multnomah, 1996), p. 121.
2. See Louis A. Barbieri, *First and Second Peter* (Chicago: Moody Press, 1979), p. 40.
3. See John F. Walvoord and Roy B. Zuck, eds., *The Bible Knowledge Commentary* (Wheaton: Victor Books, 1985), p. 30.
4. A.C. Gaebelein, *What the Bible Says About Angels* (Grand Rapids: Baker Books, 1993), p. 55.
5. For a full list of the prophecies that deal with the coming of the future Redeemer, see the appendix in my book *Christ Before the Manger: The Life and Times of the Preincarnate Christ* (Grand Rapids: Baker Books, 1992).
6. Gaebelein, *What the Bible Says About Angels,* p. 65.
7. Herbert Lockyer, *All the Angels in the Bible* (Peabody, MA: Hendrickson, 1995), p. 104.
8. Leon Morris, *The Gospel According to John* (Grand Rapids: Eerdmans, 1987), p. 815.
9. Gaebelein, *What the Bible Says About Angels,* p. 81.
10. Ibid., p. 67.

Chapter 11—Servants of the Most High

Epigraph. Millard J. Erickson, *Christian Theology* (Grand Rapids: Baker Books, 1987), p. 441.

1. Nancy Gibbs, "Angels Among Us," *Time,* December 29, 1993.
2. Cited in Cecelia Goodnow, "An Angel on Your Shoulder: More Mortals Are Getting a Boost from the Beyond," *San Francisco Examiner,* August 25, 1993, p. C7.
3. Cited in Kenneth L. Woodward, "Angels: Hark! America's Latest Search for Spiritual Meaning Has a Halo Effect," *Newsweek,* December 27, 1993, pp. 54-55.

4. Joan Wester Anderson, *Guardian Angels: True Stories of Answered Prayers* (Chicago: Loyola Press, 2006), p. 146.
5. Terry Lynn Taylor, *Messengers of Love, Light and Grace* (Novato, CA: Kramer, 2005), pp. 19, 35, 120, 148.
6. Terry Lynn Taylor and Mary Beth Crain, *Angel Courage: 365 Meditations and Insights to Get Us Through Hard Times* (New York: HarperCollins, 1999), q.v. January 10, March 20, June 12.
7. See Geoffrey W. Bromiley, ed., *Theological Dictionary of the New Testament* (Grand Rapids: Eerdmans, 1990), p. 14.
8. John Calvin, *Institutes of the Christian Religion*, ed. John T. McNeill, trans. Ford Lewis Battles (Philadelphia: Westminster Press, 1960), 1.14.11.
9. Charles C. Ryrie, *Basic Theology* (Wheaton: Victor Books, 1986), p. 133.
10. Tony Evans, *The Truth About Angels and Demons* (Chicago: Moody Press, 2005), p. 14.
11. C. Fred Dickason, *Angels, Elect and Evil* (Chicago: Moody Press, 1978), p. 12.
12. Bernard Ramm, "Angels," in *Basic Christian Doctrines,* ed. Carl F.H. Henry (Grand Rapids: Baker Books, 1983), p. 66.
13. Erickson, *Christian Theology,* p. 441.
14. G.W. Bromiley, "Angels," in *Evangelical Dictionary of Theology,* ed. Walter A. Elwell (Grand Rapids: Baker Books, 1984), p. 46.
15. Timothy Jones, "Rumors of Angels: Telling Fact from Fad," *Christianity Today,* April 5, 1993, p. 21.
16. Calvin, *Institutes of the Christian Religion,* 1.14.12.
17. See Louis Berkhof, *Systematic Theology* (Grand Rapids: Eerdmans, 1982), p. 147.

Chapter 12—Ministers to Jesus Christ

Epigraph. Rene Pache, *The Future Life* (Chicago: Moody Press, 1962), p. 106.

1. Albert Barnes, *Barnes's Notes on the Old and New Testaments* (Grand Rapids: Baker Books, 1976), p. 248.
2. Edward Myers, *A Study of Angels* (West Monroe, LA: Howard Publishing, 1994), p. 83.
3. Laurence E. Porter, "Luke," in *The International Bible Commentary,* ed. F.F. Bruce (Grand Rapids: Zondervan, 1986), p. 1188.
4. John A. Martin, "Luke," in *The Bible Knowledge Commentary,* eds. John F. Walvoord and Roy B. Zuck (Wheaton: Victor Books, 1983), p. 205.

5. J. Dwight Pentecost, *The Words and Works of Jesus Christ* (Grand Rapids: Zondervan, 1982), p. 45.
6. The text says that "*an* angel of the Lord" appeared to Joseph, and as we have seen, this is not the same as *the* Angel of the Lord, who was a preincarnate appearance of Christ in Old Testament times. See my book *Christ Before the Manger: The Life and Times of the Preincarnate Christ* (Grand Rapids: Baker Books, 1992).
7. Millard J. Erickson, *The Word Became Flesh: A Contemporary Incarnational Christology* (Grand Rapids: Baker Books, 1991), p. 24.
8. Pentecost, *The Words and Works of Jesus Christ,* p. 55.
9. Benjamin B. Warfield, *The Lord of Glory* (Grand Rapids: Baker Books, 1974), p. 108.
10. Leon Morris, *The Gospel According to St. Luke* (Grand Rapids: Eerdmans, 1983), p. 86.
11. Spiros Zodhiates, *The Complete Word Study Dictionary* (Chattanooga: AMG, 1992), p. 429.
12. Ibid., p. 591.
13. Billy Graham, *Angels: God's Secret Agents* (Garden City, NY: Doubleday, 1975), p. 128.

Chapter 13—Angels Among *Us*

Epigraph. Billy Graham, *Angels: God's Secret Agents* (Garden City, NY: Doubleday, 1975), p. 25.

1. Victor Knowles, *Angels and Demons: Agents of God and Satan...A Biblical Study* (n.p: College Press, 1994), p. 147.
2. Cited in G.W. Bromiley, "Angels," in *Evangelical Dictionary of Theology,* ed. Walter A. Elwell (Grand Rapids: Baker Books, 1984), p. 47.
3. Cited in David Connolly, *In Search of Angels: A Celestial Sourcebook for Beginning Your Journey* (New York: Perigee Books, 1993), p. 48.
4. Graham, *Angels: God's Secret Agents,* pp. 92, 95, 15.
5. Peter Kreeft, *Angels (and Demons): What Do We Really Know About Them?* (San Francisco: Ignatius Press, 2004), p. 22.
6. Graham, *Angels: God's Secret Agents,* p. 74.
7. See William H. Baker, "Our Chariots of Fire," *Moody Monthly,* January 1986, p. 36.
8. David Jeremiah, *What the Bible Says About Angels* (Sisters: Multnomah, 1996), p. 58.

9. See Millard J. Erickson, *Christian Theology* (Grand Rapids: Baker Books, 1987), p. 435.
10. Connolly, *In Search of Angels,* p. 36.
11. Louis Berkhof, *Systematic Theology* (Grand Rapids: Eerdmans, 1982), pp. 147-48; see also Timothy Jones, "Rumors of Angels: Telling Fact from Fad," *Christianity Today,* April 5, 1993, p. 21.
12. Erickson, *Christian Theology,* p. 445.
13. John Calvin, *Institutes of the Christian Religion,* ed. John T. McNeill, trans. Ford Lewis Battles (Philadelphia: Westminster Press, 1960), 1.14.7.
14. Ibid.
15. Ibid., 1.14.11, 1.14.6, 1.14.8.
16. James Montgomery Boice, *Foundations of the Christian Faith* (Downers Grove, IL: InterVarsity, 1981), p. 170.
17. Cited in Herbert Lockyer, *All the Angels in the Bible* (Peabody, MA: Hendrickson, 1995), p. 171.
18. Ibid., p. 168.
19. Graham, *Angels: God's Secret Agents,* p. 154.
20. Ibid., pp. 148, 152, 155.
21. Cecelia Goodnow, "An Angel on Your Shoulder: More Mortals Are Getting a Boost from the Beyond," *San Francisco Examiner,* August 25, 1993, p. C7; Pythia Peay, "The Presence of Angels," *Common Boundary,* January/February 1991, p. 30; Marilyn Achiron, "The Halo Effect: Sophy Burnham's Alleged Encounter with a Guardian Angel," *People Weekly,* May 17, 1993, p. 75; Sophy Burnham, *A Book of Angels* (New York: Ballantine, 1990), p. 110.
22. C. Fred Dickason, *Angels, Elect and Evil* (Chicago: Moody Press, 1978), p. 37.
23. Charles Hodge, *Systematic Theology,* abridged edition, ed. Edward N. Gross (Grand Rapids: Baker Books, 1988), p. 234.
24. Graham, *Angels: God's Secret Agents,* p. 25.

Chapter 14—Angels Among *Them*

1. Cited in Susan Hall-Balduf, "Angel Aware: Graceful Stories from Heavens Afar," *Detroit Free Press,* December 15, 1993, p. 3E.
2. Terry Lynn Taylor, *Messengers of Love, Light, and Grace* (Novato, CA: Kramer, 2005), pp. 8-9.
3. Cited in Pythia Peay, "The Presence of Angels," *Common Boundary,* January/February 1991, p. 30.

4. Joan Wester Anderson, *Guardian Angels: True Stories of Answered Prayers* (Chicago: Loyola Press, 2006), p. 146.
5. Sophy Burnham, *A Book of Angels* (New York: Random House, 2004), p. 36.
6. Alma Daniel, Timothy Wyllie, and Andrew Ramer, *Ask Your Angels* (New York: Ballantine, 1992), p. 174.
7. Burnham, *A Book of Angels,* pp. 279-81.
8. See William Evans and S. Maxwell Coder, *The Great Doctrines of the Bible* (Chicago: Moody Press, 1974), p. 219.
9. See C. Fred Dickason, *Angels, Elect and Evil* (Chicago: Moody Press, 1978), p. 98.
10. Dickason, *Angels, Elect and Evil,* p. 44.
11. Cited in Billy Graham, *Angels: God's Secret Agents* (Garden City, NY: Doubleday, 1975), p. 3.
12. Peay, "The Presence of Angels," p. 30.

Chapter 15—Fallen Angels

Epigraph. Cited in Edythe Draper, ed., *Draper's Book of Quotations for the Christian World* (Grand Rapids: Baker Books, 1992), p. 543.

1. Herbert Lockyer, *All the Angels in the Bible* (Peabody, MA: Hendrickson, 1995), p. 52.
2. This view is held by numerous scholars. See, for example, Paul Enns, *The Moody Handbook of Theology* (Chicago: Moody Press, 1989), p. 292; Merrill F. Unger, *Demons in the World Today* (Wheaton: Tyndale House, 1972), p. 8; Thomas Ice and Robert Dean, *Overrun by Demons* (Eugene: Harvest House, 1990), pp. 37-57; Lewis Sperry Chafer, *Satan: His Motive and Methods* (Grand Rapids: Zondervan, 1977), p. 15; J. Dwight Pentecost, *Your Adversary the Devil* (Grand Rapids: Zondervan, 1979), chapter 1; and C. Fred Dickason, *Angels, Elect and Evil* (Chicago: Moody Press, 1978), p. 118.
3. See John F. Walvoord and Roy B. Zuck, eds. *The Bible Knowledge Commentary* (Wheaton: Victor Books, 1985), p. 1283.
4. Charles C. Ryrie, *Basic Theology* (Wheaton: Victor Books, 1986), p. 142; see also Pentecost, *Your Adversary the Devil,* p. 11.
5. Ice and Dean, *Overrun by Demons,* p. 40.
6. Ibid.
7. Walvoord and Zuck, *The Bible Knowledge Commentary,* p. 1283.
8. Donald Grey Barnhouse, *The Invisible War* (Grand Rapids: Zondervan, 1965), pp. 26-27.
9. Walvoord and Zuck, *The Bible Knowledge Commentary,* p. 1061.

10. Dickason, *Angels, Elect and Evil,* p. 130.
11. Ibid., p. 133.
12. Ryrie, *Basic Theology,* p. 145.
13. See Dickason, *Angels, Elect and Evil,* p. 134.
14. Ryrie, *Basic Theology,* p. 145.
15. Ice and Dean, *Overrun by Demons,* p. 46.
16. Dickason, *Angels, Elect and Evil,* p. 122.
17. Charles Hodge, *Systematic Theology,* ed. Edward N. Gross (Grand Rapids: Baker Books, 1988), p. 235.
18. Ray C. Stedman, *Spiritual Warfare* (Waco: Word Books, 1976), p. 22.
19. Henry C. Thiessen, *Lectures in Systematic Theology* (Grand Rapids: Eerdmans, 1981), p. 142.
20. Lewis Sperry Chafer; cited in Ice and Dean, *Overrun by Demons,* p. 60.
21. Thiessen, *Lectures in Systematic Theology,* p. 142.
22. Charles C. Ryrie, *Balancing the Christian Life* (Chicago: Moody Press, 1978), p. 124.
23. Charles C. Ryrie, *A Survey of Bible Doctrine* (Chicago: Moody Press, 1980), p. 94.
24. Ryrie, *Basic Theology,* p. 147.
25. Ryrie, *Balancing the Christian Life,* p. 124.
26. See Clinton E. Arnold, *Powers of Darkness: Principalities and Powers in Paul's Letters* (Downers Grove, IL: InterVarsity, 1992), chapter 7.
27. Enns, *The Moody Handbook of Theology,* p. 294.
28. This is the view of Enns, *The Moody Handbook of Theology,* p. 294
29. See Ryrie, *Basic Theology,* p. 159.
30. Merrill F. Unger; cited in Thiessen, *Lectures in Systematic Theology,* p. 141.
31. Unger, *Demons in the World Today,* p. 28.
32. Millard J. Erickson, *Christian Theology* (Grand Rapids: Baker Books, 1987), p. 450.
33. Ryrie, *Basic Theology,* p. 159; see also Unger, *Demons in the World Today,* pp. 15-16.
34. See Ryrie, *Basic Theology,* p. 159; see also Arnold, *Powers of Darkness,* pp. 65-67.
35. See Charles C. Ryrie, *You Mean the Bible Teaches That...*(Chicago: Moody Press, 1976), p. 99.

36. Tony Evans, *The Truth About Angels and Demons* (Chicago: Moody Press, 2005), p. 41.
37. See Enns, *The Moody Handbook of Theology,* p. 297.
38. Cited in Enns, *The Moody Handbook of Theology,* p. 298.
39. See Erickson, *Christian Theology,* p. 449.
40. Cited in Enns, *The Moody Handbook of Theology,* p. 298.
41. See Ice and Dean, *Overrun by Demons,* pp. 119-20.
42. See Ice and Dean, *Overrun by Demons,* chapter 8; Berit Kjos, *A Wardrobe from the King: 8 Studies on the Armor of God* (Wheaton: Victor Books, 1992).
43. Stedman, *Spiritual Warfare,* p. 114.
44. Erickson, *Christian Theology,* p. 449.

Chapter 16—Anticipating Eternity

Epigraph. Cited in Edythe Draper, ed., *Draper's Book of Quotations for the Christian World* (Grand Rapids: Baker Books, 1992), p. 180.

1. Erich Sauer, *From Eternity to Eternity* (Grand Rapids: Eerdmans, 1979), p. 30.
2. David Jeremiah, *What the Bible Says About Angels* (Sisters, OR: Multnomah, 1996), pp. 17-18.
3. Hope MacDonald, *When Angels Appear* (Grand Rapids: Zondervan, 1982), p. 27.

Bibliography

1. Christian Books on Angels

Dickason, C. Fred. *Angels, Elect and Evil.* Chicago: Moody Press, 1978.

Evans, Tony. *The Truth about Angels and Demons.* Chicago: Moody Press, 2005.

Gaebelein, A.C. *What the Bible Says About Angels.* Grand Rapids: Baker Books, 1993.

Garrett, Duane. *Angels and the New Spirituality.* Nashville: Broadman and Holman, 1995.

Graham, Billy. *Angels: God's Secret Agents.* New York: Doubleday, 1975.

Jeremiah, David. *What the Bible Says About Angels.* Sisters, OR: Multnomah, 1996.

Knowles, Victor. *Angels and Demons.* n.p.: College Press, 1994.

Kreeft, Peter. *Angels (and Demons).* San Francisco: Ignatius Press, 2004.

Lockyer, Herbert. *All the Angels in the Bible.* Peabody, MA: Hendrickson, 1995.

MacArthur, John F. *The Glory of Heaven: The Truth About Heaven, Angels, and Eternal Life.* Wheaton: Crossway, 1996.

MacDonald, Hope. *When Angels Appear.* Grand Rapids: Zondervan, 1982.

Myers, Edward. *A Study of Angels.* West Monroe, LA: Howard Publishing, 1994.

Northrup, L.W. *Encounters with Angels.* Wheaton: Tyndale House, 1993.

Wiersbe, Warren, compiler. *Classic Sermons on Angels.* Grand Rapids: Kregel, 1998.

2. Books by Modern Angel Enthusiasts

Anderson, Joan Wester. *Guardian Angels: True Stories of Answered Prayers.* Chicago: Loyola Press, 2006.

Anderson, Joan Wester. *Where Angels Walk.* New York: Ballantine, 1992.

Burnham, Sophy. *A Book of Angels.* New York: Ballantine, 2004.

Burnham, Sophy. *Angel Letters.* New York: Ballantine, 1991.

Connolly, David. *In Search of Angels: A Celestial Sourcebook for Beginning Your Journey.* New York: Perigee, 1993.

Daniel, Alma, Timothy Wyllie, and Andrew Ramer. *Ask Your Angels.* New York: Ballantine, 1992.

Freeman, Eileen Elias. *Touched by Angels: True Cases of Close Encounters of the Celestial Kind.* New York: Warner, 1993.

Goldman, Karen. *Angel Voices.* New York: Simon and Schuster, 1993.

Guideposts editorial staff, compilers. *Angels in our Midst.* New York: Galilee Doubleday, 2004.

Howard, Jane M. *Commune with the Angels.* Virginia Beach: A.R.E. Press, 1992.

Piper, Don, with Cecil Murphey. *90 Minutes in Heaven.* Grand Rapids: Revell, 2004.

Price, John Randolph. *The Angels Within Us.* New York: Fawcett Columbine, 1993.

Ronner, John. *Do You Have a Guardian Angel?* Murfreesboro, TN: Mamre Press, 1993.

Ronner, John. *Know Your Angels.* Murfreesboro, TN: Mamre Press, 1993.

Smith, Robert C. *In the Presence of Angels.* Virginia Beach: A.R.E. Press, 1993.

Taylor, Terry Lynn. *Answers from the Angels.* Tiburon, CA: H.J. Kramer, 1993.

Taylor, Terry Lynn. *Creating with the Angels.* Tiburon, CA: H.J. Kramer, 1993.

Taylor, Terry Lynn. *Guardians of Hope.* Tiburon, CA: H.J. Kramer, 1992.

Taylor, Terry Lynn. *Messengers of Light.* Tiburon, CA: H.J. Kramer, 1990.

Taylor, Terry Lynn. *Messengers of Love, Light, and Grace.* Novato, CA: H.J. Kramer, 2005.

Taylor, Terry Lynn, and Mary Beth Crain. *Angel Courage.* San Francisco: HarperSanFrancisco, 1999.

3. Theology Books that Include Angelology

Bancroft, Emery H. *Christian Theology.* Grand Rapids: Zondervan, 1976.

Berkhof, Louis. *Manual of Christian Doctrine.* Grand Rapids: Eerdmans, 1983.

Berkhof, Louis. *Systematic Theology.* Grand Rapids: Eerdmans, 1982.

Boice, James Montgomery. *Foundations of the Christian Faith.* Downers Grove, IL: InterVarsity Press, 1981.

Buswell, James Oliver. *A Systematic Theology of the Christian Religion.* Grand Rapids: Zondervan, 1979.

Calvin, John. *Institutes of the Christian Religion.* Ed. John T. McNeill. Trans. Ford Lewis Battles. Philadelphia: Westminster Press, 1960.

Chafer, Lewis Sperry. *Systematic Theology,* 2 vols. Wheaton: Victor, 1988.

Chafer, Lewis Sperry, and John F. Walvoord. *Major Bible Themes.* Grand Rapids: Zondervan, 1975.

Enns, Paul. *The Moody Handbook of Theology.* Chicago: Moody Press, 1989.

Erickson, Millard J. *Christian Theology.* Grand Rapids: Baker Books, 1987.

Evans, William; and S. Maxwell Coder. *The Great Doctrines of the Bible.* Chicago: Moody Press, 1974.

Henry, Carl F.H., ed. *Basic Christian Doctrines.* Grand Rapids: Baker Books, 1983.

Hodge, Charles. *Systematic Theology.* Ed. Edward N. Gross. Grand Rapids: Baker Books, 1988.

Hodges, A.A. *Outlines of Theology.* Grand Rapids: Zondervan, 1972.

Lightner, Robert P. *Evangelical Theology.* Grand Rapids: Baker Books, 1986.

Ryrie, Charles C. *Basic Theology.* Wheaton: Victor, 1986.

Ryrie, Charles C. *A Survey of Bible Doctrine.* Chicago: Moody Press, 1980.

Strong, Augustus Hopkins. *Systematic Theology.* Old Tappan, NJ: Revell, 1979.

Thiessen, Henry Clarence. *Lectures in Systematic Theology.* Grand Rapids: Eerdmans, 1981.

4. Helpful Commentaries

Barclay, William. *The Gospel of John.* Philadelphia: Westminster Press, 1956.

Barnes, Albert. *Barnes' Notes on the Old and New Testaments,* 2 vols. Grand Rapids: Baker Books, 1977.

Beckwith, Isbon T. *The Apocalypse of John.* Grand Rapids: Baker Books, 1967.

Bruce, F.F. *The Book of Acts.* Grand Rapids: Eerdmans, 1986.

Bruce, F.F. *The Epistle to the Hebrews.* Grand Rapids: Eerdmans, 1979.

Bruce, F.F. *The Gospel of John.* Grand Rapids: Eerdmans, 1984.

Bruce, F.F., ed. *The International Bible Commentary.* Grand Rapids: Zondervan, 1979.

Cole, R. Alan. *Exodus: An Introduction and Commentary.* Downers Grove, IL: InterVarsity Press, 1973.

Eadie, John. *A Commentary on the Greek Text of the Epistle of Paul to the Colossians.* Grand Rapids: Baker Books, 1979.

English, E. Schuyler. *Studies in the Epistle to the Hebrews.* Neptune, NJ: Loizeaux Brothers, 1976.

Gaebelein, A.C. *The Gospel of Matthew.* Neptune, NJ: Loizeaux Brothers, 1977.

Gabelein, Frank E., ed. *The Expositor's Bible Commentary.* Grand Rapids: Zondervan, 1978.

Hendriksen, William. *Exposition of the Gospel According to John.* Grand Rapids: Baker Books, 1976.

Henry, Matthew. *Commentary on the Whole Bible.* Grand Rapids: Zondervan, 1974.

Jamieson, Robert, A.R. Fausset, and David A. Brown. *A Commentary—Critical, Experimental, and Practical—on the Old and New Testaments.* Grand Rapids: Eerdmans, 1973.

Keener, Craig S. *The IVP Bible Background Commentary: New Testament.* Downers Grove: InterVarsity Press, 1993.

Keil, C.F., and Franz Delitzsch. *Biblical Commentary on the Old Testament,* 9 vols. Grand Rapids: Eerdmans, 1954.

Keller, Philip. *A Shepherd Looks at Psalm 23.* Grand Rapids: Zondervan, 1976.

Kidner, Derek. *Genesis: An Introduction and Commentary.* Downers Grove: InterVarsity Press, 1967.

Lenski, R.C.H. *First Corinthians.* Minneapolis: Augsburg, 1961.

Lenski, R.C.H. *First Peter.* Minneapolis: Augsburg, 1961.

Lenski, R.C.H. *Hebrews.* Minneapolis: Augsburg, 1961.

Lenski, R.C.H. *The Interpretation of St. John's Gospel.* Minneapolis: Augsburg, 1961.

Leupold, H.C. *Exposition of Genesis.* Grand Rapids: Baker Books, 1980.

Lightfoot, J.B. *St. Paul's Epistles to the Colossians and to Philemon.* Grand Rapids: Zondervan, 1979.

Lindsey, Hal. *There's a New World Coming.* Santa Ana, CA: Vision House, 1973.

MacArthur, John. *Hebrews.* Chicago: Moody Press, 1983.

MacArthur, John. *The Superiority of Christ.* Chicago: Moody Press, 1986.

Morris, Leon. *The First Epistle of Paul to the Corinthians,* Tyndale New Testament Commentaries. Grand Rapids: Eerdmans, 1976.

Morris, Leon. *The Gospel According to John.* Grand Rapids: Eerdmans, 1971.

Morris, Leon. *The Gospel According to St. Luke.* Grand Rapids: Eerdmans, 1983.

Moule, H.C.G. *Studies in Colossians and Philemon.* Grand Rapids: Kregel, 1977.

Newell, William R. *Hebrews: Verse by Verse.* Chicago: Moody Press, 1947.

Pfeiffer, Charles F., and Everett F. Harrison, eds. *The Wycliffe Bible Commentary.* Chicago: Moody Press, 1974.

Pink, Arthur W. *Exposition of the Gospel of John.* Swengel, PA: Bible Truth Depot, 1945.

Robertson, A.T. *Word Pictures,* 7 vols. Nashville: Broadman, 1930.

Robinson, Haddon W. *Psalm Twenty-Three.* Chicago: Moody Press, 1979.

Shedd, William G.T. *Romans.* New York: Scribner, 1879.

Stedman, Ray C. *Hebrews.* Downers Grove: InterVarsity Press, 1992.

Toussaint, Stanley D. *Behold the King: A Study of Matthew.* Portland, OR: Multnomah, 1980.

Vincent, Marvin R. *Word Studies in the New Testament,* 4 vols. Grand Rapids: Eerdmans, 1975.

Walvoord, John F. *Daniel: The Key to Prophetic Revelation.* Chicago: Moody Press, 1981.

Walvoord, John F. *The Revelation of Jesus Christ.* Chicago: Moody Press, 1980.

Walvoord, John F., and Roy B. Zuck, eds. *The Bible Knowledge Commentary,* 2 vols. Wheaton: Victor, 1985.

Westcott, Brooke Foss. *The Epistle to the Hebrews.* Grand Rapids: Eerdmans, 1974.

Wuest, Kenneth S. *Wuest's Word Studies,* 4 vols. Grand Rapids: Eerdmans, 1953.

5. Helpful Reference Works

Bromiley, Geoffrey, ed. *International Standard Bible Encyclopedia,* 4 vols. Grand Rapids: Eerdmans, 1986.

Brown, Colin, ed. *The New International Dictionary of New Testament Theology,* 3 vols. Grand Rapids: Zondervan, 1979.

Brown, Francis, S.R. Driver, and Charles A. Briggs. *A Hebrew and English Lexicon of the Old Testament.* Oxford: Clarendon, 1980.

Douglas, J.D., ed. *The New Bible Dictionary.* Wheaton: Tyndale House, 1982.

Draper, Edythe, ed. *Draper's Book of Quotations for the Christian World.* Grand Rapids: Baker Books, 1992.

Elwell, Walter A., ed. *Evangelical Dictionary of Theology.* Grand Rapids: Baker Books, 1984.

Elwell, Walter A., ed. *Topical Analysis of the Bible.* Grand Rapids: Baker Books, 1991.

Kittle, Gerhard, and Gerhard Friedrich., eds. *Theological Dictionary of the New Testament.* Abridged by Geoffrey W. Bromiley. Grand Rapids: Eerdmans, 1990.

Leon-Dufour, Zavier, ed. *Dictionary of Biblical Theology.* New York: Seabury Press, 1983.

Tenney, Merrill C., ed. *The Zondervan Pictorial Encyclopedia of the Bible,* 5 vols. Grand Rapids: Zondervan, 1978.

Vine, W.E., Merrill F. Unger, and William White, Jr. eds. *Vine's Expository Dictionary of Biblical Words.* Nashville: Thomas Nelson, 1985.

Zodhiates, Spiros. *The Complete Word Study Dictionary.* Chattanooga: AMG, 1992.

6. Books on the Person and Work of Jesus Christ

Erickson, Millard J. *The Word Became Flesh.* Grand Rapids: Baker Books, 1991.

Geisler, Norman. *To Understand the Bible Look for Jesus.* Grand Rapids: Baker Books, 1979.

McDowell, Josh, and Bart Larson. *Jesus: A Biblical Defense of His Deity.* San Bernardino: Here's Life, 1983.

Pentecost, J. Dwight. *The Words and Works of Jesus Christ.* Grand Rapids: Zondervan, 1982.

Rhodes, Ron. *Christ Before the Manger: The Life and Times of the Preincarnate Christ.* Grand Rapids: Baker Books, 1992.

Walvoord, John. *Jesus Christ Our Lord.* Chicago: Moody Press, 1980.

Warfield, Benjamin B. *The Lord of Glory.* Grand Rapids: Baker Books, 1974.

Warfield, Benjamin B. *The Person and Work of Christ.* Philadelphia: Presbyterian and Reformed, 1950.

7. Books on the Person and Work of Satan

Arnold, Clinton E. *Powers of Darkness: Principalities and Powers in Paul's Letters.* Downers Grove, IL: InterVarsity Press, 1992.

Chafer, Lewis Sperry. *Satan: His Motive and Methods.* Grand Rapids: Zondervan, 1977.

Ice, Thomas, and Robert Dean. *Overrun by Demons.* Eugene, OR: Harvest House, 1990.

Pentecost, J. Dwight. *Your Adversary the Devil.* Grand Rapids: Zondervan, 1979.

Stedman, Ray C. *Spiritual Warfare.* Waco: Word, 1976.

Unger, Merrill F. *Demons in the World Today.* Wheaton: Tyndale House, 1972.

If you have any questions or comments, feel free to contact Reasoning from the Scriptures Ministries.

RON RHODES

Reasoning from the Scriptures Ministries

PHONE: 214-618-0912
EMAIL: ronrhodes@earthlink.net
WEB: www.ronrhodes.org

Free newsletter available upon request

Other Great Harvest House Books by Ron Rhodes

BOOKS ABOUT THE BIBLE

The Big Book of Bible Answers
Bite-Size Bible® Answers
Bite-Size Bible® Charts
Bite-Size Bible® Definitions
Bite-Size Bible® Handbook
Commonly Misunderstood Bible Verses
The Complete Guide to Bible Translations
Find It Fast in the Bible
The Popular Dictionary of Bible Prophecy
Understanding the Bible from A to Z
What Does the Bible Say About… ?

BOOKS ABOUT THE END TIMES

40 Days Through Revelation
Cyber Meltdown
The End Times in Chronological Order
Northern Storm Rising
Unmasking the Antichrist

BOOKS ABOUT OTHER IMPORTANT TOPICS

5-Minute Apologetics for Today
1001 Unforgettable Quotes About God, Faith, and the Bible
Angels Among Us
Answering the Objections of Atheists, Agnostics, and Skeptics
Christianity According to the Bible
The Complete Guide to Christian Denominations
Conversations with Jehovah's Witnesses
Find It Quick Handbook on Cults and New Religions
The Truth Behind Ghosts, Mediums, and Psychic Phenomena
What Happens After Life?
Why Do Bad Things Happen If God Is Good?

THE 10 MOST IMPORTANT THINGS SERIES

The 10 Most Important Things You Can Say to a Catholic
The 10 Most Important Things You Can Say to a Jehovah's Witness
The 10 Most Important Things You Can Say to a Mason
The 10 Most Important Things You Can Say to a Mormon
The 10 Things You Need to Know About Islam
The 10 Things You Should Know About the Creation vs. Evolution Debate

QUICK REFERENCE GUIDES

Halloween: What You Need to Know
Islam: What You Need to Know
Jehovah's Witnesses: What You Need to Know

THE REASONING FROM THE SCRIPTURES SERIES

Reasoning from the Scriptures with Catholics
Reasoning from the Scriptures with the Jehovah's Witnesses
Reasoning from the Scriptures with Masons
Reasoning from the Scriptures with the Mormons
Reasoning from the Scriptures with Muslims

LITTLE BOOKS

Little Book About God
Little Book About Heaven
Little Book About the Bible

To learn more about Harvest House books and to read sample chapters, visit our website:

www.harvesthousepublishers.com